PROFIT
BY
DESIGN

How to build a customer portfolio
full of profitable promoters

Includes
17 Bonus
Templates

MARK
HOCKNELL

First published in 2019 by Hambone Publishing
Melbourne, Australia

A catalogue record for this
book is available from the
National Library of Australia

NATIONAL
LIBRARY
OF AUSTRALIA

Typesetting and Design by Eggplant Communication
Cover Design by Daniela Flórez L
Editing by Mish Phillips and Stephanie Ayres

For information about this title, contact:
Mark Hocknell
mark@markhocknell.com
www.markhocknell.com

ISBN 978-0-6482011-5-1 (paperback)
ISBN 978-0-6482011-6-8 (ebook)

ENDORSEMENTS

"In *Profit by Design*, Mark Hocknell makes a compelling case for putting the customer at the forefront of your strategies, and lays out a practical method for understanding, nurturing, and enhancing the two-way exchange of value with your customers."

Evan Douglas, Professor of Entrepreneurship, Griffith University

"Mark provides a powerful framework to truly understand your customers, allowing you to design an experience which delivers immense value to them while returning a well-deserved profit to your business."

Adam Franklin, CEO Bluewire Media, Best-selling author of *Web Marketing That Works*

"Mark is great leader in customer centricity designing win-win scenarios where customers have wonderful experiences and business owners grow profitable businesses"

Jon Hollenberg, Founder 5x5Marketing, and author of *Love at First Site*

"This book made me fall in love with customers all over again! Mark helps us see the focus of business where it should be all along: the customer. Designing business from there ensures not only enduring profit, but enduring value for both the business owner and the people they serve. It's the people stuff that makes the business stuff work best!"

Zoë Routh, Leadership and People Stuff Expert, author of *Composure*, *Moments*, and *Loyalty*

"*Profit by Design* will prove to be a great addition to your sales and marketing toolkit. Mark shares his lessons learned over the past 20 years, explaining why you need a customer strategy in your business as well as how to design, implement and measure it for success. B2B, B2C or even non-profit organisations will all benefit from Mark's wisdom."

Mark Brand, Director Turing Point Partners;
Director APAC RavenHouse Asia Pacific

"*Profit by Design* outlines Mark's wealth of experience in helping businesses achieve their customer-centric agenda, taking you on that journey using his practical and pragmatic approach to growing customer value that lasts. It's worth the read!"

Michael Berndt, Chief Customer Experience Officer, eHealth Queensland

"Many organisations have expressed their intent to be customer centric, but have struggled to bring this to life within traditional organisational approaches. Other than the few exceptions, consumers generally remain underwhelmed with the value they are provided and as a result are disloyal to brands. In response to this mismatch of intent and impact, Profit by Design maps a pragmatic, step by step approach to providing value to customers that in turn drives profit for the organisation. Easier said than done in today's complex operating environments."

Steve Waters, Executive General Manager - Sales & Marketing,
Endeavour Foundation

"Mark is one of the original 'customer-focussed' professionals who has worked across many brands, organisations and teams to orient their focus, work and delivery around value creation for customers which in turn ALWAYS delivers value for organisations! Mark has shared some great ideas and approaches in this new book to update and adapt the tried and tested principles of customer value and centricity into a new era for business performance."

Tracey McFarland, Chief Experience Officer, Goodstart Early Learning

"If customers are not at the centre of how we design our business – the products and services, the structures and processes, and the culture - then sooner or later we'll find it on a downward spiral. But Mark's approach for how to put customers at the centre of our businesses creates a virtuous cycle fed by the goodness of our relationships with our customers. First, we make things better for our customers. Then, they make things better for our business through their loyalty and advocacy. And then we can continue to make more things better for more customers. Profit by Design should be the canvas on which any new or evolving business strategy is designed."

Stacey Barr, Performance Measure & KPI Specialist, Author of "Prove It!", and "Practical Performance Measurement"

ACKNOWLEDGEMENTS AND THANKS

The journey that has produced Profit by Design is the one that has accompanied me during my professional career. For that reason, there are so many people that have contributed, challenged and listened to these ideas. From the hundreds of students at the Brisbane Graduate School of Business (QUT) to scores of people in dozens of organisations that engaged me to help them find their own way to greater value in their customer portfolios. Not to mention the authors of so many books over the years that that have helped assemble these pieces together. Below is a (possibly incomplete) list of people that have accompanied me on this Profit by Design journey. Thank you.

Alicia Eltherington
Angela Devine
Barbara Landsberg
Bev Constable
Craig Wilson
Evan Douglas
Gareth Horton
Garry Marchant
Glen Richards
Jack Ferguson
James Bright

Mark Muir
Martin Hanna
Michael Berndt
Michael Lloyd
Michael O'Leary
Nicole Herbertson
Paul Davidson
Paul Davies
Paul Smeaton
Peter Hyne
Richard Ponsonby

James Charlesworth
Jennifer Gates
Joe Liang
Joeri Timmermans
Jon Kleinschmidt
Kelly Hurtz
Kelly Spencer
Kerry Taylor
Kevin Hessey
Kristy (Lee) McGrath
Mark Lourigan

Rob Mansfield
Sonya Edbrooke
Stacey Barr
Steve Baxter
Steve Goldsworthy
Steve Travis
Steve Waters
Teifi Whatley
Wendy Boyd
Wendy Joy

CONTENTS

Introduction		*x*
Chapter One	CUSTOMER PORTFOLIOS	1
Chapter Two	THE GENESIS OF PROFIT BY DESIGN	11
Chapter Three	HOW DID WE END UP HERE?	24
Chapter Four	BUSINESS ALIGNMENT WITH CUSTOMER INTENT	40
Chapter Five	HOW TO BUILD YOUR CUSTOMER STRATEGY	50
Chapter Six	VALUE FOR THE BUSINESS FROM CUSTOMERS	63
Chapter Seven	CUSTOMER VALUE PROPOSITIONS	74
Chapter Eight	THE DELIVERY OF VALUE	92
Chapter Nine	ENGAGING CUSTOMERS	109
Chapter Ten	IMPLEMENT YOUR CUSTOMER STRATEGY WITH PURPOSE	125
Appendix		*138*
Templates		*153*
Notes and references		*155*
About the author		*159*

INTRODUCTION

Welcome to *Profit by Design*. This book is the result of 20 years of working with organisations of all types and sizes, combined with many years of research and postgraduate teaching. I've watched so many businesses struggle to engage their target markets, and identified one common factor that always seems to be missing – meaningful exchange of value with the right customers. It was from this realisation that *Profit by Design* began to take shape and develop. The program in this book will take you all the way from selling products and services to engaging with the customers that are most likely to become profitable promoters of what you do. It will show you how to leverage two-way value exchange and build a portfolio of customers that will ensure you thrive. Want to succeed in this overstimulated marketing world? It's time to stop closing sales and start opening relationships with the right customers. It's time to stop chasing cash flow and start building sustainable profitability.

Let's have a quick look at what you'll find in each chapter. If you're already partway along your *Profit by Design* journey, you can skip ahead.

In Chapter 1 we will delve into the dichotomy between the old-world, product-centric approach and the customer-centric approach relevant for this age.

Product-centric Business Model		Customer-centric Business Model
• Aligned with the Industrial Age		• Aligned with the experience economy
• Pushes product onto the customer	**A dichotomy of opposing ideas**	• Informed, buying customers
• Tactic is to intrude and engage		• Word of mouth is compelling
• 80/20 tangible assets		• 80/20 intangible assets

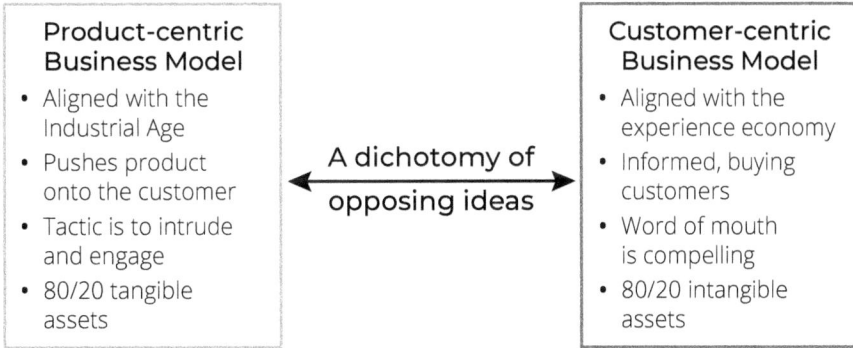

So many leaders today fail to see this dichotomy for what it is. They look to the past to see how today's large organisations successfully leveraged their products, then try to use the same strategies. When they do this, they ignore how times have changed. But more importantly, they ignore how customers have changed. Customers no longer want to be sold to. They want to buy, but they are influenced by the opinions of their social networks rather than by advertising.

Chapter 2 follows a case study that shows how the key principles of *Profit by Design* were uncovered. The case study follows a personal journey of discovery. Many people were quite shocked by the benefits of the *Profit by Design* approach, particularly since they directly challenged traditional approaches to growing value and profit. We will then see how these principles can be applied in a variety of business contexts.

Chapter 3 delves into the type of thinking that prevents so many leaders and managers from seeing what you will see. Your perception of your current constraints will become acute. Only by understanding those constraints will you be able to overcome them as you design and implement a new business model and novel strategies that will create long-term value.

From there we will go into detail on the process of using and applying the *Profit by Design* approach in your organisation. The subsequent chapters will traverse the following route, which will lead you to unlock the value in your customer portfolio – to foster a portfolio full of profitable promoters.

Build the Customer Strategy   **Deliver Customer Value**   Create a portfolio full of profitable promoters

Customer groups	→	Two-way value	→	Customer intent	→	Articulate value	→	Engagement architecture	→	Resource alignment	→

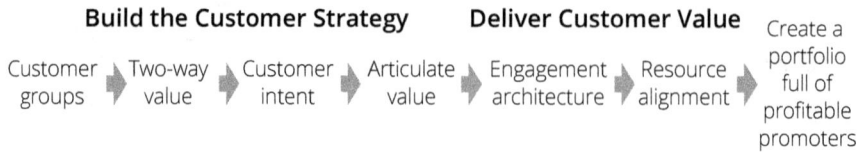

In Chapters 4 to 6, we will learn in detail how to build a Customer Strategy.

Our ultimate aim is to create a profitable portfolio of customers, so we will start there. Not all customers are equal, so we will need to examine the various customer groups. This goes beyond segmentation to really understanding how our customers behave and interact with our products and services. This will deepen our understanding of the two-way value exchange: what value the customer group gets from you, and what value you get from them. Primarily, the value businesses seek from customers is financial and advocacy, which are both measurable.

Once we know the customer groups and understand the two-way value exchange, we can then determine our intent for each group. Do we want this customer group to grow? Do we want to change how this customer group interacts with us to bring the two-way value exchange back into balance? This analysis and decision making will form our Customer Strategy – how we plan to build a profitable portfolio.

In Chapters 7 to 9, we will hone in on ways to identify and deliver customer value.

Once we know the customer portfolio we want to build and the value those customers seek, we then have to design a strategy for delivering that value. This starts with considering how we communicate value to specific groups of customers. We will see that, for customers, value propositions exist at various levels. Therefore, we will design a customer communication strategy that aims to clearly articulate value at all the various levels required.

When it comes to how we engage with the various customer groups, we will need to look at service design and an Architecture for Customer Engagement. These design elements will be the foundation of the

Customer Strategy, the basis for realising the intent of creating a portfolio of profitable promoters. Of course, this will be an iterative process. We must be sure to use action learning cycles to continually finetune the customer portfolio.

Finally, Chapter 10 will wrap the program up with some helpful approaches to implementation and change. We will use a maturity model to help you assess where you are now as a starting point for your own mission to get out of the dark, product-centric age and into the light of a business model that delivers value both for customers and for your organisation.

Next, you'll find a super-handy appendix that walks you through real-world case studies of the implementation of *Profit by Design*. In an effort to help you see more clearly how the *Profit by Design* approach can be applied to any customer context, the appendix contains three cases: a B2B case, a B2C case, and a non-profit, government agency case. As an added bonus, at the end of the book you'll find a collection of all the templates you'll need to build your own Customer Strategy.

Thanks again for joining me on this expedition of discovery. We will begin on territory that pioneers have forged, but you will soon discover this is an iterative journey where you create your own territory and map. All you need is an adventurous spirit and a positive attitude to learning and improvement.

Let's start!

CHAPTER ONE
CUSTOMER PORTFOLIOS

The central theme of *Profit By Design* is that the overwhelming value for any organisation comes from the configuration of its customer portfolio. Your customer portfolio is your unique collective of customers. How these various customers behave drives the value and cost elements that produce your financial outcomes. Some customers will get more value from you than you can recover from them. Other customers will get the value you deliver and return value. Your customer portfolio is the total sum of those customers – the pluses and the minuses.

In this book, we will discuss how to unlock the value within your customer portfolio. That means creating or building a customer portfolio full of customers that are profitable and promote what you do. Once you learn to see businesses and organisations in this way, the strategic choices involved in creating more value will become much clearer, and the outcomes will be measurable.

But first, we need to discuss what prevents leaders and managers from seeing value creation this way. For many leaders, the well-trodden paths to 'success' have resulted in rigid mindsets that, in this age, are becoming less and less meaningful. So to understand how we got to where we are today, and how things have changed, let's start with a story from the Industrial Age.

The Wedgwood empire

Let me introduce you to Josiah Wedgwood, an English potter and entrepreneur born 'poor into the squalor and dirt of a peasant industry' in 1730.[1] In his early days, products were made and bought locally in market towns and sometimes carried further afield by various merchants and traders. But by the time of his death in 1795, his name (brand) was known around the world for running one of the 'finest industrial concerns in England'.[2] He was worth £500,000.

Wedgwood was the first to produce product catalogues and put them in the hands of travelling salesmen. These salesmen travelled first throughout the British Isles, then into Europe, and ultimately right around the world. Wedgwood also had elegant showrooms with offerings like, 'Buy one get one free' and 'Free delivery for orders over £50!' Wedgwood was able to sell his products at a premium price, in large part thanks to what we would now call celebrity endorsements. Wedgwood went to great lengths to become the British Queen's potter, and later gained endorsement from the Queen of Russia.

Wedgwood was able to leverage all the technological and organisational advances that the Industrial Revolution provided, such as division of labour and industrialisation itself. These efforts not only improved the quality of the products he produced, but also the volume. And this was a hallmark of the Industrial Age. Pre-industrialisation entrepreneurs made and produced goods at a much smaller scale and really only exchanged or sold these goods locally. Industrialisation brought about a new problem for entrepreneurs: *How do we move the volume of product we can now make*? While Wedgwood was no doubt a talented potter and industrialist, what sealed his ultimate success was that he applied himself to solving this very problem: how to move large volumes of product. He was a pioneer of what we now call sales and marketing.

The Wedgwood business continued to outperform its rivals by developing and applying sales and marketing practices that are still popular today. The business was purchased in 1986 by the Waterford Glass Group for

US$360 million and now trades under the name Waterford Wedgwood, continuing to thrive even today.

No doubt about it, the sales and marketing approach Wedgwood developed to move product worked – and it worked for over 200 years. It *still* works to some extent, particularly for organisations like Apple or Coke that have high brand recognition and serious volumes of product. However, the product-centric approach that Wedgwood built his empire on no longer works for the majority. The world has changed – but businesses are yet to catch up. Yes, the technology has changed. Yes, many organisations are now digitised. But more importantly, people have changed – in how they feel about businesses and, importantly for this discussion, in how they behave as customers. It is the changes in customer behaviour that have triggered the need for new insights into how businesses can gain better value through better design of the customer portfolio.

Customers have changed

These last 10 to 15 years have seen a complete change in the way customers behave. This isn't just about the Digital Revolution or the proliferation of apps, though that has of course contributed. This is about a change in *how* customers buy. A huge portion of customer buying journeys are completed without any interaction with the people in the business. And even in those journeys that do require interaction with a salesperson, about 60–70% of the journey is completed before the interaction even occurs. It appears that we don't need travelling salespeople with catalogues anymore!

What customers need and want from businesses has changed. *When* they need it has changed. And *how* they need it (the experience) has also changed. Yet most leaders and managers haven't really adapted their customer engagement practices to align with the way new customers engage and buy today. We may have added some self-service tools or catalogues to websites, but many of the old product-centric sales and marketing tactics are still being used.

There are probably many ways you've seen customer behaviour change, in yourself and others. Here are the top five ways I've noticed that customers have changed.

Customers are sales resistant

No one wants to be sold to. Anything that looks like, sounds like, or feels like *selling* will make the customer's resistance rise. Back in Wedgwood's day, products were new and information was shared by word of mouth, so salespeople were indispensable. But these days, after decades of dodgy sales practice and stereotypically pushy sales behaviours, people don't want to talk to anyone, let alone someone they think is pushing them to buy purely out of self-interest. In short, customers have had enough of being sold to.

Customers want to do it themselves

The widespread resistance to selling has triggered a self-service revolution. It seems the optimal experience for a customer today is not when they can access the experience and advice of someone from the business to help them make a decision, but when they can make the decision themselves. If they want advice, typically they will check in with their large and connected social networks. A customer today can ask their online social network about the best local Indian restaurant or what car they should buy, and within moments have the information they sought direct from a trusted source... which leads us on to the next point.

Customers have more information available to them than ever before

Scattered across the internet are endless expert reviews from 'independent' sources that have done the comparisons for you and, even more importantly, reviews and comments from other customers – real people, just like you, with no bias (well, not much). Customers will do their research, read other people's reviews, ask around, and then decide for themselves. As bestselling author Dan Pink puts it, sales people are needed when there is "information asymmetry, where the seller always has more information than the buyer." The sales person knows more than the buyer and the buyer needs to ask someone about the product, service or solution provided.[3] In many contexts today however, the buying customer knows more than the person selling, particularly when it comes to what other customers are saying about their products.

Customer expectations are rising

No matter what type of organisation or business you are in, the expectations your customer has of you are now much higher than ever, and increasing. Customers expect that things should be easy. They expect you to get it right. They expect you to know them. Some businesses have really nailed the customer experience, which has made our expectations as customers rise even further – often to the point where the service and experience many other organisations provide seems, by comparison, 'clunky' and 'unprofessional' or, on the other end of the scale, overly professional and not human enough. Either way, it's not what the customer expected, and as far as they're concerned, it's not good enough. At this point the customer is likely to disengage, or at worst spread negative word of mouth to their networks about your organisation.

Customers are joining the experience economy

As we have become less and less satisfied with product-based consumerism and raised our expectations of service providers, the economy has shifted to one where customers are making their purchasing and advocacy decisions on their overall experience. We all could probably identify half a dozen examples where we have spent money based on the experience – our favourite coffee shop or restaurant, or perhaps a Wedgwood tea set for Mum. And whether or not we advocate a product is definitely based on our overall experience. But the experience economy is also manifesting on a more macro level.[4]

Consider the music business. Not that long ago music artists and bands made records/CDs and then went on tour to promote sales of their albums. Today, artists produce digital music and songs that are easily accessible and cheap or free. They produce music so that when they go on tour their legion of fans come to the show. This is where the majority of the money now is for these artists: concert tickets. What does the customer buy...? An experience. They buy expensive tickets to hear the same songs they have on their phones because it's an *experience*. Clearly, this industry has transitioned to the experience economy.

———

Since the turn of the century, our customers have completely changed how they behave. This has brought about – or at least stimulated the beginning of – a different economy that's much less about consuming products and much more about having experiences. Customers will make their decision to spend/invest with your organisation, or to provide positive word of mouth for your organisation, based on how you make them *feel* – not what information you provide. And yet so many organisations and businesses today continue to rely on the 'tried-and-true' sales and marketing methods from a hundred years ago to create their customer portfolio.

Profit by Design provides a pathway and a set of techniques that will help you deliberately build a customer portfolio that provides value for your customers and, in turn, increased long-term value for your organisation.

Let's first look into this dichotomy between an approach focused on products and an approach focused on the customer portfolio.

The product-centric approach

Many businesses focus on what they *do* – the services they provide, the products they make – in the belief that sales and revenue lead to profitability for the business. Again, this thinking comes out of the Industrial Age, when the 'problem' was about selling products to people who, for the most part, had never seen products like these before and were learning new things about them as they were being sold. During the last century, armies of door-to-door salespeople took to the streets to sell their products, from brushes and cleaning products to 24-volume encyclopaedias (that also came with a free bookcase!). These salespeople had a lot more information about these new products than the customer, especially in terms of their features and benefits. Obviously, this is far from true in today's retail landscape.

Product-centric thinking leads businesses to focus on developing the product, as well as keeping an eye on competitors and product alternatives. But selling lots of product does not directly increase profitability for the business. It can, but it often doesn't. A focus on the product misleads business leaders into driving sales and marketing teams to sell more, generate revenue, and worry about profit later. This effectively compartmentalises the business functions, creating silos and factions rather than interdependent, collaborative teams. The marketing team succeeds when it produces an agreed quota of leads for the selling teams, or produces enough mass brand awareness to push enquiry levels up to a certain level. Likewise, the sales team succeeds when it meets pre-agreed and negotiated quotas. The causal relationship between individual team performance and overall organisation success is tenuous at best. Often teams become self-serving and live in survival mode – where one team can win while another loses – rather than working towards a common business outcome.

A product-centric mindset can also lead us to thinking that products sell themselves. We give the customer all the information we can think of – features, benefits, and random testimonials are listed ad nauseam. The reality is: products do not sell themselves. Products are 'sold' when a customer decides to buy. More products are sold when a customer was so pleased with the product or service and experience that they tell others, who also buy. Additional products are purchased based on the first customer's initial experiences with those products and services.

Using a product-centric mindset and approach today in your business or organisation will limit the value you can create.[5] Selling more product does not lead to greater value creation for the business, especially if you are selling to the wrong customers. What *will* lead to great value creation for the business itself in the long term is focusing on value creation for your customers.

Let's now define the customer portfolio and look into how it generates value. In the next chapter, we'll look into the story of where these principles first came to life for me.

The value of the customer portfolio

Profitability for a business is a direct outcome of the customer portfolio. Whether we are talking about for-profit businesses (large, medium or small), government-owned corporations, or not-for-profit organisations, the value they create is the sum of the customer portfolio. Put simply, the customer portfolio (or customer base) is the cumulative sum of your customers – the number and the value of those customers. This will, of course, change over time as you gain and lose customers. The value of a given customer is their individual margin – revenue earned through the customer, less the cost to serve.

Each year, you (hopefully!) retain a certain portion of your customers. This means that the financial value of each customer depends not only on what they are spending now, but also on what they will spend in future. (On this basis, we can calculate an *estimated Customer Lifetime Value*, or eCLV – more about this later). For example, if you gain 100 new customers in year one and retain customers at 80%, then in year two you will still have 80 of these customers; in year three you will still have 64, and so on. Are these customers paying subscription fees, renewing products, or repurchasing from you? And what are the ongoing costs to serve these customers? Your customer portfolio is made up of the customers you acquire and the customers you retain. It is the net sum of your customers, today and into the future.

The ongoing value of the customers in your customer portfolio is the value of the business. Each customer has a lifetime value, calculated based on their individual margin and the overall retention rate. Adding the lifetime values of all your customers gives an overall financial value of your customer portfolio. But it's vitally important not to only consider the numbers. Today, the financial measure is only part of the value from your customer portfolio.

Advocacy within your customer portfolio is a key driver of business profitability. Word of mouth has always been critically important for business, but today it is paramount. What percentage of your customer portfolio actively promote your products and services to their friends, colleagues, and family? What percentage of customers actively provide negative word of mouth? The level of advocacy within your customer portfolio has a critical impact on the number of customers you retain, as well as the number and cost of newly acquired customers. High levels of negative word of mouth can increase service costs, acquisition costs, and losses. But it's worth noting that this is always relative to the alternatives available to your customers. For example, some 'telcos' have a high percentage of customers giving negative word of mouth (detractors), but they may not be that concerned as long as the alternative telcos have just as many or more detractors. We'll discuss customer advocacy in more detail later.

Most businesses have an ongoing relationship with their customers, and this is where most of the ongoing revenue comes from. Customer behaviour motivated by the ongoing relationship – that is, repurchasing and word of mouth – is a significant driver of the profitability of the customer portfolio. If your business standard is to produce a one-off sale with no further relationship then you might feel like you are in a slightly different position, and you are – but your success is still reliant on customer behaviour.

Since its introduction to online businesses in the late 1990s, customer feedback has become ever more important. Now, almost every business has an online presence, and customer reviews drive search results and significantly influence customer decision making. Most of us wouldn't dream of booking accommodation for a holiday or interstate business trip without first checking the reviews of other customers (or getting a recommendation from a friend). The level of advocacy within your customer portfolio is a key contributor to the value of your customer portfolio.

In short, the value of the business is derived from the customer portfolio – it is the cumulative value of every customer. That value, a combination of the dollar value and the word-of-mouth value, is a predictor of the future value of the business. Business leaders should see groups of customers as revenue streams and recognise that different customer groups offer different kinds of value to the business. We will examine these concepts in far more detail in subsequent chapters.

Summary

We started by looking into the Industrial Age origins of sales and marketing. Why? Because many businesses build their customer portfolios mainly through their sales and marketing efforts. This is a product-centric approach to thinking about business growth, and it is fast approaching its use-by date. Relying on this approach nowadays will lead to a whole range of shortcomings in business model design and implementation. Customers have changed how they behave. We are entering into an experience economy, in which the long-term value of a business or organisation comes from the configuration of its customer portfolio. This value is derived from both the financial value of customers and the advocacy they provide.

CHAPTER TWO
THE GENESIS OF
PROFIT BY DESIGN

As my *Profit by Design* journey began, there were not only lessons I had to learn about the value of the customer portfolio, but also paradigms I had to unlearn and let go. I was guided by one overriding fact: the value of the customer portfolio is persistent and profound. Above all, I discovered just how important it is for the organisation as a whole to focus on how the customer portfolio is created, rather than allowing all the various teams and individuals, each with their own unique perspective, to do what they feel is best. Focusing the whole organisation on *how* the customer portfolio is created – rather than letting it happen by chance – is the key driver of long-term value. We will finish this chapter with the three key insights I learned about how businesses create their customer portfolio almost unwittingly.

Lessons from financial services

I feel that I intuitively first learned these principles many years ago as a young lad working for my parents' businesses, but the definitive lessons came while working for a financial services group a few years ago.

The financial services group I worked with was divided into three product 'houses': a bank, a general insurance company, and a wealth management business. From a regulatory and business perspective, each product house was assessed on its financial results. The bank's profits came from the deposits it collected and the loans it disbursed, such as property loans, personal loans, and credit cards. The insurance company produced an underwriting result: net profits from insurance premiums collected less claims paid out on, for example, home and car insurances. Finally, the wealth management business made money based on sales of financial planning services, investment products, and life and income protection insurances. Yes, this is a little oversimplified, but I think you get the point: each product house made money from the products it sold, less the costs outlaid.

In the early 2000s, this financial services group decided to implement a Customer Relationship Management (CRM) system.[6] I had a background of working across many distribution channels and was appointed as the business lead on this initiative. We began by looking at the technology systems that would support our goal of having a CRM system. The project soon grew into a program as we started to piece together all the components required to make CRM successful. We would need an operational CRM system, supported by a single customer database, a way to do activity-based costing, and marketing systems and analytics. The first step was to create a single customer database, which would form the foundation for a clear Customer Strategy that could be brought to life by people across the group. With around two million customers across multiple product systems (with no consistent naming conventions and duplicate customers everywhere), creating this database was a project in itself.

The program ran continuously for more than three years, deploying a suite of six core pieces of technology in a sequenced delivery. The change affected 5,000 employees. The story of the program is a story within itself, but for our purposes, the point is that the seeds of success were sown with a deep understanding of the customer. As we looked deeper into the customer portfolio, the unexpected insights we uncovered eventually led to a group-wide cross-selling approach that would result in the highest cross-selling rate of any financial services organisation in Australia.[7]

———

So what were these customer insights that we stumbled across? To start with, we recognised that our customers generally purchased as a household. Decisions about financial products and services were typically made together, either as a couple or as a family unit. A child's first banking products normally followed along with the household banking. Likewise, when a child got their first car, it would likely be insured by the same insurer that the household used. It therefore made sense to analyse households, not individuals, as the basic customer 'unit'.

It's important to recognise the flaw in averages. We knew that the average value of a household to the group was about $680 per annum, but this doesn't provide any actionable insight whatsoever! To work out where customer value was coming from, we needed to break the portfolio down into segments.

We divided the customer portfolio into five segments based on the annual value contribution of the household. Ideally we would have used an estimated customer lifetime value, but back then we weren't that sophisticated! We analysed profit contribution per annum, but also recognised that customer retention was a key driver of long-term value.

This is what the five segments looked like:

Segment	Average Profit Contribution per Annum	Percentage of Total Customer Portfolio (Approx.)
A	> $2,600	14%
B	$1,000–2,600	
C	$100–999	57%
D	$0–99	29%
E	< $0	

Pareto's 80/20 principle was alive and well here in this customer portfolio – 80 percent of value was coming from around 20 percent of customers (households).[8] This reflects one of the key principles of the customer-centric approach to business: not all customers are equal. When I talk with businesspeople today, they readily accept this principle and do recognise that potentially 80% of their customers aren't adding much value at all.

In the late 1990s, a couple of Australian banks realised this principle as well, and determined to 'sack' a lot of customers they no longer wanted.

They closed the accounts of these low-value customers, and even closed some of the branches that were serving them. The backlash from the public was huge (actually, I believe this is where the term 'bank-bashing' stems from). The problem, though, was that the banks weren't reducing their costs in line with the amount of customers they were sacking. Although the profit per customer increased, so did the cost per customer – thereby reducing the overall profitability of the customer portfolio.

When we recognise that a significant portion of customers may not be adding much value to the business, the reaction shouldn't be to get rid of those customers, but to ask different questions. What is it that makes our more valuable customers more profitable? Why are we acquiring new customers that are not profitable? How do we turn our less valuable customers into more valuable, or at least cost-neutral ones?

Diamonds in the portfolio

As we delved into the customer portfolio, we expected to find that the valuable customers were also the high-net-worth clients. But this was not the case. High-net-worth clients are great to win over, but they can be more costly to serve and often seek discounts. When we looked into customer engagement and spending in more detail, we found that a particular type of customer/household was associated with a higher value to the organisation. Around 40% of these customers were in Segment A, another 35% in Segment B, and 25% in Segment C. The average profit contribution of these segmented households was $2,767 per annum. We called these 'Diamond Customers'.

A Diamond Customer had at least five products and was engaged across at least two lines of business (banking, insurance, and/or wealth management). They had utilised service channels that cost less to serve, and leveraged value from linkages between their products, like transfers for loan payments or insurance payments. These customers had not only engaged in a way that delivered value for the organisation, they had also extracted more value from the business for themselves. It was this symbiotic, two-way exchange of value that made these customers absolute diamonds.

While the financial services group itself managed and assessed each line of business – insurance, banking, and wealth management – separately, the customers saw it completely differently. They saw an organisation that offered a range of services and products that they could use to manage their finances, protect their assets, plan for the future, and improve their quality of life. This was something of a surprise to us at the time. But there were two other surprises that topped it off.

First, we looked at the retention rate of customers. We found that the average retention rate for a customer of a single line of business, let's say insurance, was about 80%. The Diamond Customers, on the other hand, were retained at a rate of about 98–99%. These customers were invested in the relationship they had developed with the company. They had connected with the brand and with its array of services. In other words, we would have to do something really bad to lose one of these customers!

Retention of customers adds significant monetary value to an organisation. The estimated lifetime value of a customer contributing $2,000 per annum and retained at 80% is $5,714 (using a discount rate of 8%; more on this later.) For a customer with the same annual contribution, but a retention rate of 98%, the estimated lifetime value is $19,600.

Second, we conducted further research into the Diamond Customers. What we found was that these customers were highly likely to give positive word of mouth to their family and friends. It turned out that not only were they making decisions to engage with the products and leverage the services to extract value for themselves, they were also advocating to others to do the same. When your customers are advocates of what you do, attracting the optimal customer is that much easier.

For me this was the first profound example of a two-way exchange of value. A subset of customers, invisible to the business until now, was extracting optimal value from the organisation, while also delivering value for the business. As the Diamond Customers leveraged the products and services to gain value, the business was rewarded with higher levels of profitability through margins, retention, and promoter behaviour.

Insights into action

Once we understood *how* value was created for the Diamond Customers, we could then develop tactics to create more customers with the same characteristics. The overall strategy was to grow the number of Diamond Customers. Therefore, we needed to retain our existing Diamond Customers, convert as many other existing customers into Diamond Customers as possible, and encourage all new customers to be Diamond Customers. By growing the number of Diamond Customers, we would increase the profitability of the customer portfolio.

First, we considered how to retain our existing Diamond Customers. We found that one of their key frustrations was that the organisation did not really treat them as a group customer – interactions were always based on a single line of business (banking, insurance, or wealth management). Every time the customer moved house and wanted to change their mailing address, they had to contact each part of the organisation individually to update their details. Therefore, we decided to deliver the capability to update customer details across all the product systems with a single action. This was implemented in the final phase of the program.

Converting existing customers into Diamond Customers came down to a cross-selling strategy. First, we needed buy-in from frontline employees. This was achieved through educating everyone about what Diamond Customers were and how much value *they* were getting from the organisation. Frontline people care about the people they interact with and need to feel they are adding value. So to engage frontline people, we had to demonstrate value for the customer, not just the business.

Next, we educated frontline employees as to what each customer needed in order to become a Diamond Customer, which was as much about leveraging the value of existing services as it was about adding products. Real-time marketing systems also helped with producing these 'next-best-offers' that were focused on adding value for customers (either service suggestions or products) with the ultimate goal of creating more Diamond Customers. Additionally, the executives in charge of the bank, insurance, and wealth management product houses not only accepted financial targets, but also committed to grow the portion of their customer portfolio that had other products with the group, which drove higher levels of cross-product collaboration.

When it came to customer acquisition, a few things had to change in order to onboard new customers as Diamond Customers. For example, the bank's lenders were predominantly assessed and rewarded based on loan disbursement – the dollar value of loans drawn down from the bank. From a customer perspective, applying for and getting a loan from a bank to purchase a new car, home, or investment property is a fairly big life event. Lots of information is exchanged, including future goals and plans. Yet the business was really only interested in dollar drawdowns and conducting the transaction efficiently. The insights we gained about Diamond Customers indicated that this needed to change. Much more could be done to offer customers better value not just from the loan, but also from related financial services. Processes, systems, and incentives were changed to align with the goal of onboarding all new customers as Diamond Customers.

After all these initiatives were implemented, the organisation had the highest cross selling rate of any financial institution in Australia. We grew the number of Diamond Customers, significantly improving the profitability of the customer portfolio, and built the organisational capability to continue achieving this for years to come. Incredibly, the CRM program achieved a return on investment of more than 100% within a mere 12 months.

Lessons learned

As we explored the customer portfolio for the first time, we found that the way customers behaved significantly affected the profitability of the customer portfolio in ways the business never expected. We also discovered that the thinking of the people who ran or managed the organisation was very much framed by what they saw, failing to take into account what they couldn't see.

This whole experience provided a significant and profound set of lessons for me. Throughout my work both at the time and with a broad range of organisations, I have found that a few specific principles are consistent across all industries and sectors, in business-to-consumer and also business-to-business contexts. The common theme? People.

The three key lessons were:

1. Customer portfolios are *created* by the business – through implicit and explicit actions and decisions.

2. Not all customers are equal. Customers differ in how they gain value from the business, and in how they reciprocate value (typically margins, retention, and advocacy).

3. Most organisations cannot see their *awesome customers* – those that represent the optimal value to them and that are getting the best value from their offerings.

Now that we have seen how these 'lessons' applied to a large financial services customer portfolio, let's take a quick look at each one and see how it might apply across other contexts.

Customer portfolios are created by the business

Since working with the financial services group, I have collaborated with more than 50 other organisations. Every time I've looked into an organisation's customer portfolio, I've found similar mixes of customer groups, each representing different levels of value to the business. And every time, as these differences in customer groups become obvious, someone asks, 'How did we get here?' In the following section we will discuss in more detail the systematic process by which we can identify meaningful customer groups. But for now, let's look at a couple of real-world examples and see how something that seems like a good idea at the time can actually leave a business with a customer portfolio that's less profitable than before.

A subscription software business provides a software package for building contractors that allows them to quote jobs and then manage costs and variations as the job progresses. The software also incorporates a financial system that meets the regulatory obligations for managing subcontractors and tax compliance. This product solves a key problem for contractors, who typically quote in Microsoft Excel, manage delivery of the job through a project application, and take care of financials through yet another system.

To gain more sales, the company decided at the outset to set their price quite low. Before long, they ended up with a customer portfolio full of people who weren't really committed to setting the software up, and weren't reaping the full benefits. Frustrated staff would often comment, 'We know our customers are not using the functionality, but we can't get them to use it!' These customers did not provide positive word of mouth, they were reluctant to renew their subscriptions, and they required much effort (and cost) to try to retain. The business had created their customer portfolio through poor decision making, which led to actions that reduced profitability.

The solution was to raise the price commensurate with the value of the software, develop the ability to communicate this value, then ensure that each new customer set up the system in a way that ensured they got the maximum value from their subscription. Over time customer retention and advocacy increased, and cost to serve reduced.

This is how the two-way value exchange works in practice. We must ensure that if we claim a set of benefits for customers, they receive those benefits – in bucketloads. By ensuring customers get absolute value, we increase the value of the customer portfolio.

Let's consider another example of a business inadvertently reducing the profitability of their customer portfolio. I worked with a building supplies company that wanted to grow their sales. They had a large national network of salespeople visiting existing customers, as well as an internal (inbound) sales team taking orders from existing customers.

It was decided that the outside sales team needed an incentive to get more customers. So, a target – to add one new customer each month – was linked to their bonus/commission structure. Seems reasonable, right? Not too onerous on the salespeople. However, this was a very mature market. All the potentially valuable customers knew them or had dealt with them in the past and had, for one reason or another, chosen not to be a customer (maybe they chose another supply partner or had poor credit). The salespeople met the target of getting one new customer per month quite easily... by going to smaller, less valuable customers. They added them into the system and took an order, thereby meeting their target and growing the customer portfolio. However, many of these smaller customers had actually already been getting product from the business, just indirectly through their larger customers. The customer portfolio grew, as did the cost of acquisition – but overall profitability did not, and nor did advocacy.

Not all customers are equal

Each customer is different in how they gain value from the business, and in how they reciprocate value (typically through margin, retention, and advocacy). The secret is in grouping these customers in meaningful ways that help us understand and leverage this value exchange.

First, let's note that the Diamond Customers within the financial services group found a way to gain value from the products and services that was almost beyond the imagination of the business, particularly from a product-centric mindset. In turn, they reciprocated much more value than other customers.

Likewise, in the case of the subscription software business, a handful of customers figured out how to use the full functionality of the product. They had invested their time and effort into setting everything up and learning how it works, and had the discipline to apply the processes to their own businesses. The value they gained from the software was huge. They were confident on the margins they would make from their contracts, and regulatory compliance was achieved with the click of a mouse. They were advocates for the software, and had a retention rate of 100%.

Yet when the business wanted to grow the customer portfolio, they offered their product to new customers at a low price point. These customers did not have the commitment to learn how to set up the system and expected everything to be much easier that it actually was. Most did not resubscribe. Nor were they advocates for the system – why would they be, when they had tried to use it and could not get the promised benefits?

The software business could see their awesome customers, but they failed to recognise them. They took the approach that it was up to the customer to get the value from the product, and it was this thinking that prevented them from growing the profitability of their customer portfolio. Not all customers are equal, and to grow the profitability of the customer portfolio we need to ensure the customer gains value.

Most organisations cannot see their *awesome customers*

We saw in the case of the financial services group that the Diamond Customers – the most profitable customers – were initially hidden from view. The building supplies company was in a similar situation. They were having high levels of interaction with a group of customers that were really 'wheelers and dealers' – price-sensitive customers who just wanted a cheap deal. We found that these customers, who accounted for about 15% of the customer base, were taking up a lot more time and effort than other customers, and had a lower margin. Their idea of advocacy was bragging to others about the deal they got, rather than giving actual positive word of mouth for the business.

We looked within the customer portfolio to discover customers that were interested in a partnership style of relationship. These customers valued service and consistency of supply, potentially outsourcing some inventory management to their supplier. These customers offered higher margins and an ongoing partnership – which in this context related to retention and a high share of wallet. By focusing more effort on these customers, and leaving the 'wheelers and dealers' to their competitors, this business improved the profitability of their customer portfolio.

Another example of this principle arose when I worked with an operator of passenger rail services along the coastline of the state, and between the coast and regional centres. They were keen to grow sales and get more people using their passenger services, and to them the obvious target was backpackers. They were planning a huge international campaign to attract more backpackers. This did seem like a good idea. But first we did a review of the customer portfolio. We found that backpackers did provide some value, and that word of mouth on social media influenced other backpackers to use the passenger train services. However, many were purchasing a cheap travel-pass ticket rather than individual train tickets. In the process, though, we did find another interesting customer group.

People that lived within regional areas and were looking to take a short break or visit family and friends were repeat travellers, mostly on full-price tickets. We revised our goal to instead grow this customer group. These customers were the gems within the portfolio. This didn't mean that the rail operator wouldn't also market to backpackers, it just meant taking a more balanced approach to growing the profitability of the portfolio. Through an analysis of the lifetime values of its customer groups, the company was able to determine the optimal investment in marketing to ensure a return. Finding and knowing your awesome customers allows you to finetune your customer engagement approach to improve the profitability of your customer portfolio.

Summary

The composition of a business's customer portfolio provides the best indicator of long-term profitability. The number and value of customers gives us the base value, but the retention rate allows us to also calculate value into the future. Ongoing customer relationships add value over time, particularly in an age where the value of advocacy is of utmost importance. The value of a business is derived directly from the customer portfolio – the cumulative financial value of every customer, combined with word-of-mouth value.

Always, the development of strategy and tactics should be based on improving the value of the customer portfolio – increasing the proportion of Diamond Customers.

The three key lessons I learned from my experience with the financial services group bear repeating:

1. Customer portfolios are *created* by the business – through implicit and explicit actions and decisions.
2. Not all customers are equal in how they gain value from the business, or in how they reciprocate value.
3. Most organisations cannot see the *awesome customers* that represent optimal value to them and to their customers.

These three insights are key to designing your business for profit.

CHAPTER THREE
HOW DID WE END UP HERE?

Having looked at where the value for organisations comes from – their customer portfolios – many people ask, 'So what's the problem? Surely businesses get this?' Apparently not. When you look at the majority of organisations today, the Pareto principle of 80/20 is alive and well. Around 80% of the value for most businesses is generated by only a small portion of their customer portfolio, maybe 20% or less.

In addition to taking a product-centric over a customer-centric approach to creating business value, there are many other mindsets that prevent leaders and managers from seeing how true value is created. A couple of hundred years of industrialisation have given rise to many classic business success tales that have since become traditional approaches. They worked once, so why kick against them? Well, I've said it before and I'll say it again: the world has changed.

So, what's the problem?

We talked earlier about the product-centric approach. As noted, this thinking leads organisations to believe, simplistically, that the product generates revenue, and from this revenue comes profit. In her book *Chief Customer Officer*, Jeanne Bliss describes products as one of the 'power cores' within businesses.[9] These power cores are the strength and focus of an organisation, and determine how things go. Bliss identifies six power cores that 'have the greatest impact on driving customer profitability within the organisation':

- *Product* – production and distribution of physical products or services
- *Marketing* – creation of customer engagement through advertising campaigns and tactics
- *Sales* – the process of getting 'conversions'
- *Information technology* – the actions and projects required to create capability
- *Business vertical* – the core discipline of the business that drives what happens
- *Customer* – the end user of the products, whose 'decisions emanate from understanding what will drive the greatest value to customers in the short and long terms'.[10]

When an organisation focuses on the first five power cores (or dominant thinking types), they miss the point about the value of customers and the customer portfolio. I worked with a timber sawmilling business that had the majority of its resources – human, technological, and financial – focused on the task of creating timber products. Try mentioning customer needs or value and the response would be something like, 'You need to understand we are a disassembly business; we take apart the trees we are given and produce products... the customer can only take what we make.' But as we know, customer value is about much more than the product. Ultimately, the leadership of this business was able to transition to become more customer centred and profitable.

Consider what an organisation is. It's not the products it produces, nor the systems and processes that it describes in its manuals. Essentially, an organisation is a collective of people. It is the people within an organisation that bring it to life. It is the people who lead it, who make the decisions about its design and structure, and who create its culture. Even if the business is fully digitised, it is still the people in the 'lower' levels that bring the services and experiences to life. And it is the people who are customers that will eventually define its value.

The various 'power cores' within an organisation drive the predominant type of thinking of its people. The power cores create mental models within the organisation – how people think, how they solve problems, how they plan, and how they do what they do. These mental models become the culture: 'the way we do things here'.

The thinking type of the organisation drives its culture, and as management guru Peter Drucker famously quipped, 'Culture eats strategy for breakfast, every time.'[11] Likewise, the thinking within the leadership group will define the way the business is designed and operated, and ultimately the results it achieves.

Within each of us is a set of beliefs and assumptions that drives how we think as we evaluate options and decisions. We often are not fully aware of our belief systems, which have been developing in us since we were born. Neuroscientist Tali Sharot refers to our collective of beliefs and assumptions as 'priors'.[12] Most of us have a very active 'confirmation bias', which preferentially seeks information that confirms our prior beliefs. To shift or adjust these beliefs takes much more than data. When information conflicts with our established belief system, our first instinct is to reject it. A change of mindset starts with common ground – a place to start building new beliefs and rewriting some of those assumptions.

Writing this now reminds me of when I was first appointed to manage a sales contact centre. I had some experience in sales and management, and I'd read a lot on managing sales teams. One of the recurring themes was to have periodic competitions. Apparently they would lead to higher sales, as well as excitement and fun for the team. But as I ran my first competition for the team, I noticed that only a few, maybe 8 out of 45, were excited. The rest just went along with it, rode it out, and got back to normal afterwards.

A few years later I discovered the work of Alfie Kohn, in particular *The Case Against Competition*.[13] Kohn's research showed that competitions break down teamwork, as everyone is out for themselves. For the same reason, there is very little sharing of 'best practice'. When I reflected on this, I realised that I had (unknowingly) adopted the assumptions and beliefs of sales practice – to detrimental effect. It was only when I reflected on some new learning that I became aware of my bias. The next time, we ditched the league ladder and focused on everyone achieving their personal best (PB). We rewarded effort and growth; the team bonded and shared ideas and tips; and everyone improved their PB.

So now let's take a quick look at what I have found to be eight of the biggest misleading traditions (or assumptions) in sales. These assumptions often become entrenched *priors* for many leaders, managers, and entrepreneurs.

The eight misleading beliefs of sales and marketing

These misleading ideas are symbiotic. Each belief reinforces the next, exacerbating the flow-on effect: that is, is that the customer portfolio is not created deliberately. Rather, the portfolio develops somewhat by chance over time, and often becomes one where 80% of value for the business is produced by a small portion of customers – and that's if they're lucky. As you read through this list of painfully common beliefs, notice how deeply intertwined the underlying assumptions are. It's no wonder these myths are so profoundly ingrained in business.

1. Sales is easy

Sales is rarely seen as a profession. People typically do not go to university to become a salesperson, though so many science graduates end up finding work in sales roles. For example, many pharmaceutical reps have degrees in medicine, similarly with engineering and machinery sales. It is for this reason that in 2015 Griffith University in Australia developed a subject on selling and sales management (2038MKT), even making it a requirement for some courses (such as Entrepreneurship), with a view to better preparing students for productive work after graduation.

The perception that *sales is easy* leads to all sorts of poor decisions within the business. Often if sales aren't happening the way they were forecast, it's assumed that it has to be the fault of the sales team. This then leads to a range of other issues as the business tries to 'fix' the sales leader or sales team. This is a key contributor to the high turnover rates among salespeople and chief sales officers.

This perception that sales is easy leads on to the next misleading belief.

2. Build it and they will come

Too much focus on the product leads businesses to put effort into product development without even thinking about finding the right customers for the product or seeking any kind of customer input. This singular focus on the product is based on the idea that when the product is built, the customers will come.

I am constantly surprised to see start-up businesses focusing on growth, rather than *profitable* growth. I posed this curiosity to my friend and mentor Evan Douglas, Professor of Entrepreneurship at Griffith University in Australia. He explained it to me this way. Studies have shown that entrepreneurs have an expectation of sales over time that almost always exceeds reality. Even if the business starts up with the right intentions,

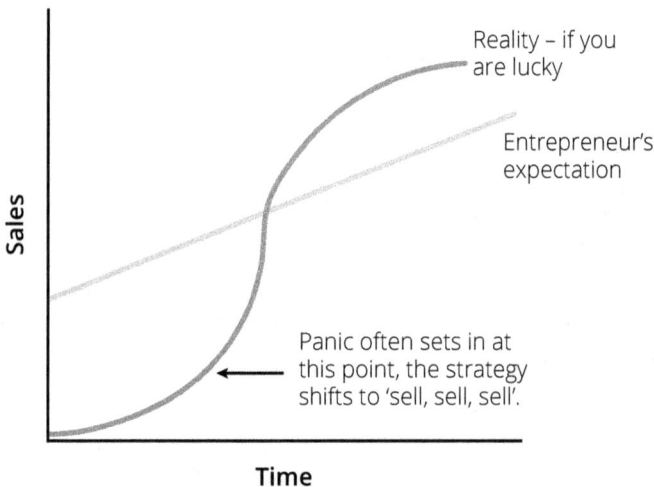

as sales fall behind expectations the focus quickly changes to generating cash flow. The sales team is encouraged to 'sell, sell, sell', which typically results in a customer portfolio where 80% of customers only contribute 20% of profit. While the business is hooked on cash flow, a large portion of its resources is invested in servicing lower-value customers. This adds to the cost base, which in turn increases the need for cash flow. And so the cycle continues, towards ever-declining levels of profitability.

Planning for profitable growth by selecting potentially awesome customers from the outset allows for a more tempered view of growth that increases the probability of creating a profitable customer portfolio. The view that you can just develop a product or service and the customers will flow in treats customer growth as no more than a numbers game.

3. It is all a numbers game

This fallacy – that if you have something to sell, then it is only a matter of the number of people you talk to – is firmly believed by many people. It's the idea behind the 'sales funnel' that is so often used to describe the leads-to-conversions process (social media, marketing, sales). Maybe it was okay as a metaphor once upon a time, but it has now stopped being useful at all. In fact, I believe this emphasis on it all being a numbers game actually hinders future customer engagement. Let me explain.

The sales funnel had its origins in the early days of the last century, when knocking on doors was key to making sales (the earliest reference I found was in 1911).[14] Nothing much changed when we evolved to making phone calls. Back then the role of salespeople was to share information with prospects who, usually, did not know about the products. So what happens today, in this age of information parity? Our customers are doing their research online and within their social networks. This accounts for up to two-thirds of their buying journey. We can try to apply the funnel to this situation – to translate the front end to include people visiting websites, downloading a report, or signing up for an email newsletter. But the reality is that this is not what the funnel was designed for. The customer environment and context has changed, and yet we are still using the same tool. This does not make any sense.

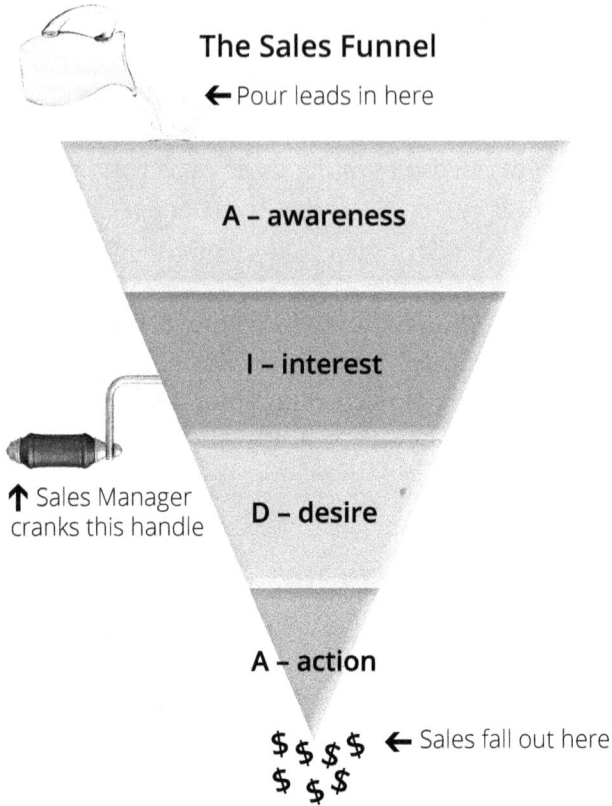

The Sales Funnel

← Pour leads in here

A – awareness

I – interest

↑ Sales Manager
cranks this handle

D – desire

A – action

$ $ $ $
$ $ $ ← Sales fall out here

The second big problem with the funnel is that it requires us to qualify
the various stages and make particular individuals or teams responsible
for each stage – the social media manager and/or marketing team for the
top and middle, and sales for the bottom. Marketing requires 'qualified'
leads from the social media part of the funnel; the sales team requires
'qualified' leads from the marketing stage. If the sales team says the
marketing team has not provided 'quality leads', the business may develop
even more complicated qualifications to govern these leads as they
pass through the funnel. There are often intense internal negotiations
between teams about these qualifications to ensure 'fairness across the
playing field' – so everyone can get their numbers. The funnel fosters
'horse trading' between internal teams that are more concerned about
getting their numbers than growing the profitability of the company.
Rather than managing the whole system, we are focused on the parts

and internal machinations. A 2013 Forrester Report demonstrates the inappropriateness of the funnel by showing that the conversion rate from top to bottom is 0.75% (for B2B in the Western world).[15] Yes, 99.25% of the people you bring into the funnel reject your offering. This seems more than a little inefficient!

Finally, the language of the funnel is a shocker. Let's think about the people that might want to engage with our brand and offerings, and especially those people we would like to become our customers, to love what we do, and to become promoters of what we do. Now, let's call these people 'leads' and describe them using terms like 'marketing qualified', or 'sales qualified'. Now, like evangelists on a mission, let's see them as unenlightened individuals that need to be converted. Is this really how we want to treat our future ideal customers? I think not. We should start the customer relationship the way we want it to be forever. How an organisation communicates through its social media, marketing, and sales teams has a huge influence on how its people think about and talk with its potential awesome customers.

The sales funnel comes from the era of door-to-door salespeople, more than a hundred years ago. Whether you were selling brushes, cleaning products, or encyclopaedias, the idea was that you just had to knock on enough doors. Today this assumption leads managers to think it is all about the numbers, when the reality is that it is far more about truly understanding your ideal customers, knowing how to find them, and preparing for and having genuine conversations with them.

4. The sales gun

This is a classic hero tale. Sales managers are struggling to get their products to market. Then, all of a sudden, along comes a 'sales gun'. Immediately, everything changes! The sales gun brings in busloads of customers and sells masses of product. Eventually, the sales gun rides off into the sunset (with huge commissions) looking for the next business to save, leaving the first business none the wiser as to how it was done. And so the hunt begins for another sales gun.

I am continually stunned by the number of businesses that tell me their sales strategy is to 'get a sales gun'. This demonstrates a basic failure to understand the factors that truly engender business success. Each business must figure out who its awesome customers are – those customers in the sweet spot of the two-way exchange of value, the profitable promoters. Once you know your awesome customers, then you can develop customer engagement and retention tactics to build a profitable portfolio of these customers. Deliberate and purposeful customer engagement must be a core capability of any business today. You cannot rely on an individual for success.

A sales gun is never an answer to the sales problem.

5. One throat to choke

This is an ugly term, but one that is often used. It's about managing the parts rather than the whole – holding individuals responsible for their part of the chain. The idea of 'division of labour' was developed by Adam Smith in the late 1700s, and it's still going strong.[16] Business leaders continue to advocate strong divisions between teams on the basis that if you hold one person accountable for sales, another for marketing, and another for social media, then you have single-point accountability ('one throat to choke'). This is a fantastic way to create 'silos' – environments where one team can succeed at the loss of another. It breaks down teamwork and collaboration as team leaders go into survival mode. Success is about not drawing attention to yourself and hoping someone else gets that unwanted attention.

Surely today we want product development, social media, marketing, and sales to work as a single team to engage with our awesome customers and develop a customer portfolio for the business that is profitable and full of promoters. We need to manage the *system* – to engage individuals and teams to fit together seamlessly and work towards a common goal.

6. Success means meeting targets

What does success look like? Get your numbers. Now the game is on.

When individual targets are the definition of success, most people will seek to win by any means and at any cost. This could mean selling to anyone that will buy (even if they cancel at a later date) or manipulating the numbers to hit the target.

Remember the B2B sales team that was given a target to get one new customer each month? They achieved it by approaching the customers of their larger customers. Target achieved – but with unfortunate consequences for the business. Adding these smaller customers increased costs and annoyed the larger, more profitable customers. (But nobody can deny that the salespeople achieved their target!)

Breaking down your financial plan and using this as your customer engagement strategy will fragment your intent. All the sales team will be concerned with is hitting the targets you have set, regardless of the customer. Profit for businesses comes from the value of its portfolio of customers. Condensing this down to a simple set of numbers does not work.

7. Close the sale

Sales managers often say they are looking for 'closers' – people who can close the deal and make the sale. This is another idea that thrived in the last century. Closers and deal-crunchers might have been heroes in the bygone era of the classic movie *Glengarry Glen Ross*, but not now.

Today's economy is based on people's perceptions of experience and feelings of connection. Customers are more informed about products and sales than at any other time in human history. Customers are more *sales-resistant* than ever; they are more aware and tired of the tricks salespeople and businesses use to try to cajole them into buying. Approached this way, the customer won't buy. But they will certainly tell as many people they can of their encounter with the conniving salesperson and their ultimate victory and escape!

Today the goal is not to close sales, but to open relationships with customers who will be advocates of what we do. Therefore, our behaviours and actions need to reflect our goal – and that means the old sales tricks are out.

8. Sell the product or service

This misleading assumption of sales is at the end and perhaps also the beginning of a symbiotic cycle that is all about a focus on selling things. This focus on the *selling* activity leads us to tell people (usually anyone that will listen!) all of the fabulous features of these particular products. And, yes, sometimes there is a discussion about benefits.

Today's customers are seeking value, and they define value in ways that often do not relate directly to features (we will cover this in more detail later). This insight led UK research firm CEB to develop a new approach, published as *The Challenger Sale*, where the mantra is essentially this: Don't tell your customer anything they could Google, but rather provide insights that will add value to their understanding and application of the benefits.[17]

Customers don't need to be informed by humans of product features; this information is readily available. Our conversations with customers needs to be more about the true exchange of value.

––––––––

Sales leaders, take note! Stop being deceived by these old methods and tactics. They are not relevant for this age. They are not relevant for building teams. And they are not relevant for allowing customer-facing people to focus on the experience they are delivering for the customer.

Consider instead building methods and tactics based on a simple paradigm that I like to call the 'flow of customer engagement'. Here's how it works:

Imagine you are standing alongside a pristine stream. Upstream in the distance are some potential customers. You don't quite know them yet, can't quite see them clearly. As they are drawn towards you, you start to see and understand them more clearly. Your role now is to remove the obstacles that prevent them from getting close to you. To gently draw them towards you. And, if the value exchange between you is right, and communicated well, to welcome those customers into your pool of customers (who are also your advocates).

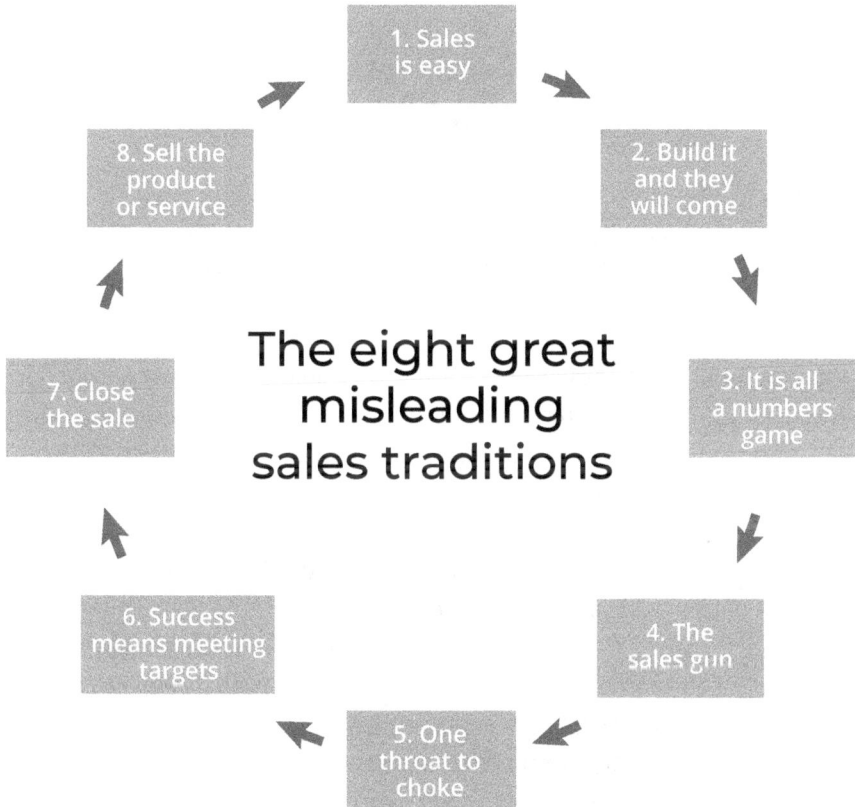

The eight great misleading sales traditions

1. Sales is easy
2. Build it and they will come
3. It is all a numbers game
4. The sales gun
5. One throat to choke
6. Success means meeting targets
7. Close the sale
8. Sell the product or service

How we are organised

To me, when it comes to building profitable customer portfolios, there seems to be a problem not just in our mindset but also in the way we are organised – the structures we create, and the way those structures interact to deliver value.

Strategy should precede structure

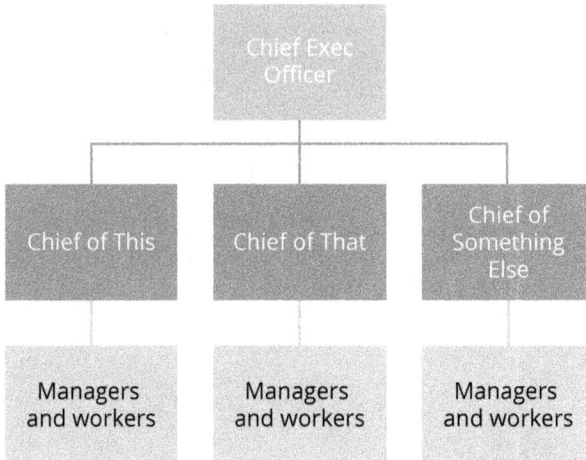

Organisational structures, even for small businesses, really reflect our history as humans. Even though most of the structures we use today were developed in the 1900s, the feudal nature of these structures seems to hark right back to the Roman Empire.

Two thousand years ago, when a citizen joined the Roman Army they swore an oath of allegiance and were then placed into a team of eight. Ten teams formed a Century, led by a Centurion with three assistants. Six Centuries formed a Cohort, and ten Cohorts formed a Legion.[18] Each Legion was led by a Legatus (a member of the Roman Senate), supported by seven direct reports that supervised the entire Legion. If we look at larger organisations today, we tend to find many similarities in team sizes and structure. However, what made the Roman Army so effective in its day was that it deployed as a synchronised unit with a clear, singular objective.

Organisations today still use these structures and ratios, but they forget about the focus on a clear, singular objective: to deliver value for customers and in return create value for the organisation. Far from following a common objective, the feudal tribes of today's businesses, while (somewhat) loyal to their chief, are all looking out for themselves. It's them against the other departments. We often hear that the marketing team has sabotaged the sales effort by suppling non-qualified leads. We hear of customer service groups and customer-facing project implementation teams deriding the efforts and ethics of salespeople. All this reinforces the tribal boundaries and highlights that each group has its own objectives, rather than working towards one collective outcome. Strategy should always precede the development of structure, and for today's businesses that means the structure must underpin the creation of the two-way value exchange.

Businesses exist for customers

From a customer's perspective, the organisation really exists for them. As far as they are concerned, airlines do not exist to build a fleet of well-maintained jets; they exist to take paying customers safely from one place to another. Insurance companies do not exist to generate huge surpluses of cash; they are there to meet the promises they have made to customers. Electronic consumer goods businesses do not exist to make the most attractive and cool technologies; they exist to meet the current and emerging needs of their customers.

All organisations exist to deliver value for their select customer groups, including non-profits. Why do local governments remove your rubbish or provide library services? It's done in return for rates and services fees. If the perception of the customer is that the value returned does not meet the price paid, the council will be held to account, publicly, in the media, and at the ballot box. Organisations exist for customers. Without customers willing to pay, there is no organisation.

Even for organisations that primarily provide products, service always constitutes part of the overall customer experience. In addition to the value that comes from explicitly stated products and services, the overall experience adds to the assimilation of value for the customer. And it is based on this perceived value and experience that customers determine whether or not to repurchase, recommend to others, and support the organisation.

Organisations exist to deliver value for their customers. They do this through the people, systems, and processes they develop. From a customer perspective, the business has to function as a coherent system that delivers value and good experiences for them.

Businesses are systems that deliver value

Everything within the business – the systems, people, functions, processes, products and services – works as a collective to deliver value. How the customer perceives this overall, collective value predicts future customer behaviour, which in turn is a significant predictor of business results. It is on this basis that the business will, over time, either thrive, survive, or go into decline.

Examining businesses this way starts with systems thinking.[19] Systems thinking is all about looking at the whole – not the individual elements, but the combination of elements. When we seek to understand how these elements interact with each other, we are using a *systems thinking* approach. This means we are thinking about relationships in a dynamic (as opposed to static) way. Metaphorically, we can think of the system as a movie as opposed to a series of photographs, or the collective output from an orchestra as opposed to the melodies of each instrument. Each musician performs individually, but, guided by the conductor, collectively they produce an emotionally stirring combination of sounds, rhythms and vibrations.

One of the key challenges all businesses face is managing the system – getting all the parts of the organisation to coordinate and collaborate so that they deploy as a synchronised unit with a clear, singular objective: to deliver value for customers. Value in this context includes the customer experience. The flow-on effect for the business of delivering customer value to the right people is a profitable customer portfolio.

Poor structural design and poor management practice join hands to create a toxic culture and embed silos and fiefdoms within organisations. In addition to lacking unity across intra-organisational boundaries, many businesses consistently fail to deliver value for their customers. In many cases if value is created, it is almost by chance rather than on purpose. If value is created for the right customers, this also is often by accident.

A business – as a system – must create value. It must create value for its chosen customers, so that those customers can in turn create value for the business, which then allows the business to continue to deliver value for their customers.

Summary

In this chapter we have considered some of the common problems affecting the creation of profitable customer portfolios, particularly the mindsets and assumptions that people bring to their roles. Organisations today are a composite of the history that has brought us to this point in time. However, we are now moving from the Industrial Age to the Digital Age. The economy has shifted to one more driven by the experience and opinions of customers.

Businesses need to align themselves around one common objective: growing a profitable customer portfolio. The system must be deliberately aligned, organised, and synchronised to deliver value for the chosen customers. And to do that, the components of the system – the structure, culture, processes, and people – must be optimised to allow the business to deliver value for their chosen customers better than anyone else.

In the following chapters we will focus on the frameworks and tools to transform and build businesses that are relevant for this age and economy. Businesses that create value for customers and themselves.

CHAPTER FOUR
BUSINESS ALIGNMENT WITH CUSTOMER INTENT

From the previous discussion it should be fairly apparent that for long-term success, a business should design its activities and align its resources to improve the profitability of its customer portfolio. Even not-for-profits and government corporations seek to create a surplus, or at least deliver more value for less. The common denominator is always the customer.

The customer-centric business model

Designing the business from the perspective of deliberately creating the customer portfolio takes place in three phases, as shown in the model opposite.

We'll come back to this model and each of the phases in more detail shortly. But for now, we can see that Phase 1 is about developing what I call a Customer Strategy. This is about knowing your customer groups and understanding the two-way value exchange. In Phase 1, you need to work out, as we did for the Diamond Customers in Chapter 2, what your intent is with each customer group. First, we will discover the customer groups by going beyond segmentation and personas to examine customer behaviours and truly understand what they need and value. Then, we can match this with an understanding of the value of these customers to the business in order to develop a clear approach to growing the long-term value of the business.

Phase 2 is about value propositions. Most businesses are skilled at telling us why we should buy products (another hangover from the Industrial Age), but very few are skilled at articulating why we should buy from *their* organisation. As humans, customers make decisions emotionally.[20] Only then do they use rational information to justify the decision.[21] As Simon Sinek says, 'People don't buy what you do, they buy why you do it.' Therefore, the Value Proposition has to be about *why* a particular customer group should engage with you. Before we even *mention* products or services, we need to connect emotionally and in a values-driven manner with our chosen customers. What common ground, values, and beliefs do you have?

Phase 3 is the part most organisations are addicted to – action! This is the *doing*, the management of inputs and outputs. The best strategy in the world is completely useless if it never gets implemented. Equally, action that hasn't been built upon the foundations of the first two phases is

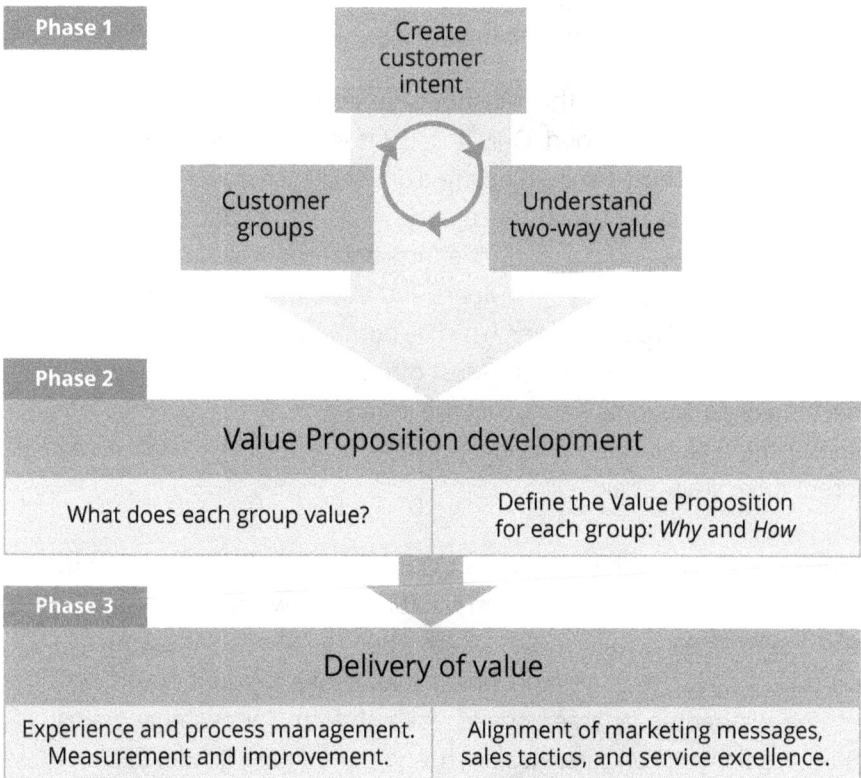

Phase 1

Create customer intent

Customer groups

Understand two-way value

Phase 2

Value Proposition development

What does each group value?	Define the Value Proposition for each group: *Why* and *How*

Phase 3

Delivery of value

Experience and process management. Measurement and improvement.	Alignment of marketing messages, sales tactics, and service excellence.

often wasted, as it does not support the overarching strategy. Yet every day, businesses spend hundreds of thousands of dollars on actions that offer them no real long-term value. Marketing messages, sales tactics, and services have to align not only with each other and with the value propositions developed in the previous phase, but also with the intent for each customer group.

The three phases have a logical feel and flow. It seems as if it ought to be easy for an organisation to work out who their awesome customers are. It seems simple enough to communicate that value in a way that resonates with these awesome customers. And it seems obvious to focus on aligning resources in an effort to build a portfolio full of awesome customers. After all, the more we align our business intent with our customers, the more value we create, and the less waste we produce. But in a product-focused world, this alignment rarely happens. Most organisations don't even take the first step towards identifying their customer groups. They send messages focused on features of products and services, rather than on real value.

The key problem here is that most businesses operate with Phases 1 and 2 completely under a cloud. Only Phase 3 is visible to them. In the place where Phases 1 and 2 should be are a financial plan and a set of targets to achieve through any tactic necessary. In the fray of day-to-day activity, leaders negotiate and barter their efforts and resources in an attempt to reach their KPIs. These behaviours and trade-offs are perceived as being connected to a 'strategy', which is normally a fairly vague outcome with a list of actions or projects. Most often, the behaviours have actually become organisational habits that are linked directly to individual KPIs and/or the financial plan or budget.[22] They have nothing to do with real intent or strategy at all.

As we saw earlier with the financial services group's Diamond Customers, there are significant benefits from focusing on how you build the customer portfolio. This holds true whether you're setting up your portfolio from scratch or improving the value of a customer portfolio you have inherited. A large body of research from, for example, Harvard Business School, Forrester Research, and the London School of

Economics demonstrates the following four primary benefits to focusing on building the customer portfolio:[23]

1. *Greater profitability*, mainly from focusing on the right customers and creating a two-way value exchange that improves retention.

2. *Greater business resilience*, especially in volatile economic conditions.[24]

3. *Greater customer engagement*, leading to improved retention and promoter behaviour (that is, a higher-value customer portfolio).

4. *Greater employee engagement*, bringing agility and improved capabilities. It's a curious thing. You get more engagement from employees when you focus their attention on creating value for customers, rather than meeting financial targets.

To begin to leverage these benefits, the organisation needs to be designed for maximising profit by improving the value of the customer portfolio. This starts with a Customer Strategy. The next chapter will demonstrate *how* to build your Customer Strategy, but for now let's look at its role within the business.

Why your business needs a Customer Strategy

There are three key reasons why your organisation needs a Customer Strategy:

1. *Product revenue does not equal business profitability.* When we deliver value for our customers, *they* become ongoing streams of revenue and advocates of what we do. Revenue is derived from customers, not products.

2. *Not all customers are equal.* Not in the value they receive, nor in the value they reciprocate to you (in the form of their financial lifetime value or advocacy).

3. *A Customer Strategy gives all staff a clear aim to work towards*, and strategies to achieve it. In the absence of a Customer Strategy, your

teams and people will instead take action to meet their individual financial targets, quotas, or KPIs, effectively fragmenting your 'strategy'.

The Cascade Equation

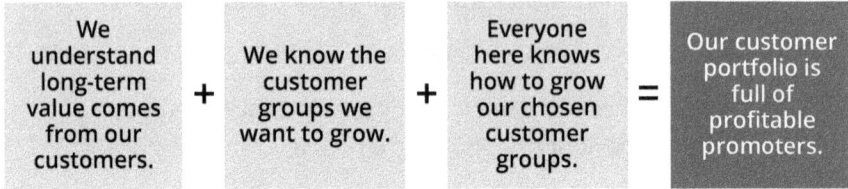

| We understand long-term value comes from our customers. | + | We know the customer groups we want to grow. | + | Everyone here knows how to grow our chosen customer groups. | = | Our customer portfolio is full of profitable promoters. |

Revenue is driven by delivery of value, not products

We often look to the number and value of products sales as being income (which it is). We often talk about products as if they have a life of their own – 'this product sells itself' and so on. However, in doing so, we forget about the customer who made the decision to buy the product.

What we know now is that, for the customer, decision making is fairly complex. It's not the rational, step-by-step process that we might imagine, but rather a far more emotive process that is deeply connected with memory.[25] This 'irrationality', if you like, on the customer's side doesn't mean that we can't build a strategy around them. However, it does mean we need to make more effort to understand their behaviours if we are to build a profitable portfolio. The number of sales is dependent on the decisions made by customers, particularly considering that most customer decisions are influenced by other customers, such as social influencers, family, friends, and colleagues. What proportion of customers in your portfolio are advocating your brand? How many are actively providing negative word of mouth?

If your customer makes repeat purchases, or they subscribe to your product or service, they are doing so based on their experiences with you and their overall perception of the value you have delivered. This value is a trade-off between their perception of benefits over sacrifices. Note that this perception may not be the objective reality, but it *is* the reality for the customer.

Value for the business comes from customers. Customers who make decisions to buy, to repurchase, and to stay with you. Customers who make the decision to tell people they know about you, about what you do, and about why you do it.

Not all customers are equal

In the financial services example in Chapter 2 we discovered a specific type of customer that represented less than 20% of the overall portfolio, yet contributed a significant portion of value back to the business. We even put a name to it: Pareto's 80/20 principle, which states that 80% of value comes from about 20% of customers. I've worked with more than 50 organisations since and found this principle to be consistent across all sectors and industries. In fact, if anything it can be more extreme, with some businesses easily getting to 90/10.

So what does this have to do with needing a Customer Strategy?

You don't want your people (even if it's with the best intentions) forming energy-consuming relationships with customers from the 80% of the customer portfolio that does not add much value. Nor do you want them establishing relationships in a way that could prevent the customer from getting the value you deliver (and therefore prevent them from reciprocating). What you do want is for your people to know which customers represent the best value and how to establish relationships with those customers based on a mutual exchange of value. The best way to do this is to build a strong understanding of your ideal (or awesome) customers – the ones that will be profitable promoters of what you do – and grow that portion of your customer portfolio. This is at the very essence of what your Customer Strategy can do for you.

Financial targets fragment strategy

All too often in leadership and management we take our lead from the Industrial Age. In those days (just last century!) it seemed like a good idea to split an organisation up into departments and sub-departments, and then hold one person accountable for the outcome (usually a financial target).

Financial targets, as you probably know, were generally related to revenue for management teams, staying within budget ('spend') for marketers and service teams, and potentially the number of units sold for sales teams.

As we know, the world has completely changed in the last 10–15 years. We have transitioned into an experience economy. Customers are different in how they behave; employees are different in how they feel at work... but rarely are employers different in how they run their organisations. Many organisations are still bogged down in figuring out the overall organisation-wide return to shareholders, or earnings per share, or gross profit, then determining the revenue and cost base required to achieve those numbers, then dividing it up across the organisation... This does not recognise where value comes from! Nor does it recognise the collective value of the sum of the parts. Most leaders are still trying to control their organisations with siloed financial targets.

As a manager, if I am provided with financial goals (budgets, targets or quotas), then my accountability for those numbers will drive my decisions about what actions to take. The stated organisation strategy might be one thing, but *my* survival depends on getting those numbers. If each manager takes the same approach, any idea of an overriding strategy (vision, mission and/or purpose) is lost. The goal is solely to hit the numbers. Across any organisation, large or small, financial goals fragment strategy.

Today more than ever, we need our teams to collaborate to achieve a single goal. Sure, teams might contribute to that goal in different ways, but we need them all working towards the same outcome. We need teams to learn and improve. We need teams to provide optimal value and experience for customers, so that those customers stay, spend more, and advocate to their friends, family, and colleagues about the value we deliver. We need to allow the Customer Strategy to *cascade* through the organisation, not fragment.

So what is a Customer Strategy?

Your Customer Strategy is a re-articulation of your Business Strategy in the context of the customer. The realisation of the goals in your Business

Strategy will come from changes in your customer portfolio. For example, almost all businesses have a goal to increase profit. But in executing this, many businesses focus on growing revenue and cutting costs as individual aspects, rather than looking at ways to increase profit as a whole. Most cost-cutting efforts focus on where most of the cost is, which is typically in the workforce. A business can more effectively increase profit by finetuning their portfolio – decreasing the portion of lower-value customers, increasing the portion of higher-value customers, changing relationship types (to improve value exchange), and growing the number of advocates.

Any Business Strategy must clearly articulate the measurable outcomes or results you seek, not just the actions. The Customer Strategy makes these business goals clear and aligns all resources to make progress towards the goals. The Customer Strategy provides guidance for effective, common-sense approaches and tactics that allow the product design, sales, service, marketing, and performance improvement teams to collaborate and work towards a single outcome – a higher-value customer portfolio.

Lots of organisations today claim to have a Customer Strategy – or member strategy, or community strategy – that puts their customer first. Often these strategies are fairly generic: 'The customer is at the heart of all our decisions', 'Everything we do is for our members', 'Products and services focus on customer benefit over profit.' These 'strategies' sound more like value or principle statements and often create more debate within the organisation than clarity. It is impossible to build alignment across the business with customer intent that is vague.

A useful Customer Strategy will:

- Identify your various customers groups, recognising their unique characteristics and how they define value differently to other groups. This will go beyond segmentation to understand the behavioural attributes that guide decision making.

- Identify what represents absolute value to each group. Remember, these customers are making decisions based on their perception of value. We need to know what this value is.

- Understand the value each customer group represents to you as an organisation. Not all customers are equal, so let's understand the differences in the types of value the valorous customers return to you.

- Seek to understand the exchange of value between your business and the customer. This should be an optimal, mutual two-way exchange – the 'sweet spot' for both you and the customer.

- State an intent or strategy for each customer group, defining which customers you want to *Grow*, *Maintain*, *Re-engineer* the relationship with, or perhaps *Retire* from the portfolio. Each intent will have the purpose of finetuning the portfolio to become more profitable.

- Develop value propositions for each customer group. Each proposition must resonate with the corresponding customer group. This will include two levels: the overarching *why* proposition and the *what* and *how* for products and services.

From these strategies and value propositions, we will then develop the optimal tactics for the business to achieve the goal of improving the value of the customer portfolio.

Summary

We looked at the three-phase model for designing the business with a deliberate focus on creating a more valuable customer portfolio. We recognised that most organisations focus only on action, the doing of the work, with only a tenuous link back to some vague strategy. All too often organisations are guided by financial plans and budgets. We also saw that since my first insights into *Profit by Design*, much corroborating research has emerged to verify these benefits.

Next, we saw how a useful Customer Strategy can guide the efforts of the business. It can ensure everyone within the organisation is focused on progressing closer and closer to a more profitable customer portfolio – towards the outcomes and results set out in the Customer Strategy.

Armed with a Customer Strategy, an organisation can better align the resources of its people, processes, and budgets to deliver value for chosen customer groups, which will in turn increase the value of the customer portfolio. When your whole team collaborates towards a common purpose for customers, you become more agile, foster learning, and improve performance. Reflect for a moment. Are you fragmenting or cascading your business strategy?

Now it's time to look at how to build a Customer Strategy.

CHAPTER FIVE
HOW TO BUILD YOUR CUSTOMER STRATEGY

There are three primary steps to building your Customer Strategy:

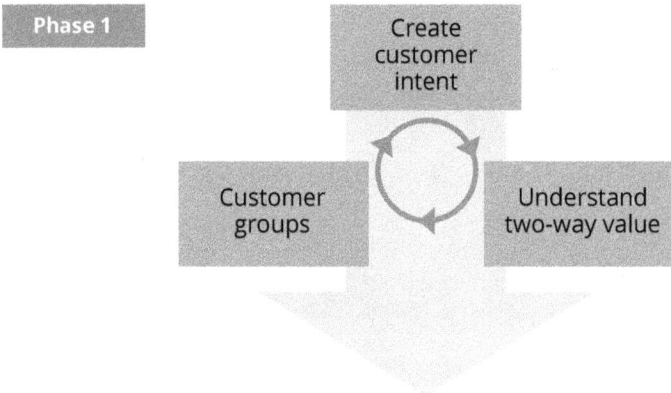

1. Define your customer groups.

2. For each group, gain an understanding of the two-way exchange of value.

3. Determine your intent for each group. Do you want to have more of these customers? Do you want to change the way the relationship works? Or is it perhaps time to let some of these customers go?

Step 1: Define your customer groups

I am deliberately not using the term 'segments' in reference to customers. When most people think of a segment they consider things like demographics (e.g. age, gender, occupation), geographics (where they live), and perhaps psychographics (e.g. social class, lifestyle). From a marketing perspective this is normally the place to start. And certainly, segments might be a good place to *start* with your customer groups – but it doesn't go far enough. You really need to take your understanding of the differences in the various groups much further.

First, create a list of the different customer groups, then consider what distinguishes one group from another. For example, Amazon have four primary (core) customer groups: Consumers, Sellers, Enterprises, and Content Creators.[26] Each group needs and values something different. Consumers want access to buy the things they like, and value recommendations from Amazon that match their interests. Sellers love the ability of Amazon to reach consumers and distribute anywhere in the world. Each core customer group then has sub-groups.

Start the process for your organisation by listing the obvious grouping of customers. Then examine what differentiates one group from another in terms of behaviours and actions. Investigate your customer groups in ever more detail. What are their attributes? What is their potential spend? How do they buy, spend, and promote? What do they value, and how do they define that value?

———

Here are a couple of illustrations.

A building supplies company frequently provides products to large contractors and merchants. The sales team regularly visits these customers to assess their current and future needs and to take orders. At first, the company split customers into groups based on whether they on-sell the products directly to their customers or repurpose the products for their customers. Each business type had different needs from similar products. Then it was recognised that processes, management systems, and disciplines typically differ between large and small businesses. Businesses were therefore categorised according to size or, more specifically, 'wallet size' – the total amount in dollars that the business could spend with the building supplies company per month. We now had customer groups based on both type of business (two groups) and wallet size (five groups, imaginatively named A, B, C, D, and E in order from large to small).

Now that we were now looking at customers in a different way, we soon discovered an attitudinal aspect that would end up defining the whole Customer Strategy. There was a perception within the sales team that 'most' customers were mainly interested in price. But when we tested this, we found that only about 15–20% were price focused, the majority were service focused, and about 25% were most interested in building a collaborative partnership. Because this was a value of the customer, not a property of the organisation or the product, it was quite easy to describe the behaviours of each group of customers.

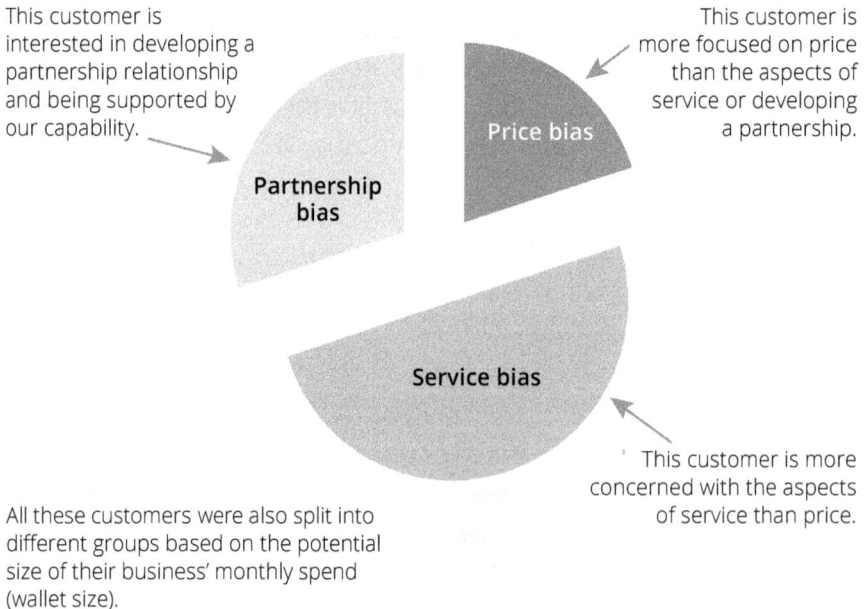

This customer is interested in developing a partnership relationship and being supported by our capability.

This customer is more focused on price than the aspects of service or developing a partnership.

Price bias

Partnership bias

Service bias

This customer is more concerned with the aspects of service than price.

All these customers were also split into different groups based on the potential size of their business' monthly spend (wallet size).

Customers were now grouped by not only type of business and wallet size, but also whether they were Price, Service, or Partnership focused. The Customer Strategy was to *Grow* the large (A and B) customers who were Partnership focused, in terms of both share of wallet and percentage value to the customer portfolio. Service-focused A and B customers were given more attention and became a source for more Partnership customers. Finally, the Price-focused customers received purely transactional service – no more wasted time trying to cut a deal with these guys!

Superannuation funds have recognised for quite some time now that segments are useful, but they're not enough. Generational groups are important to fund managers, but the attitude of the customer is even more important. In every generation, some customers will be interested and engaged in the development of their retirement savings, while others will be completely uninterested, for a variety of reasons. Different strategies are required for different attitudes even within the same demographic groups. For interested members, the organisation needs to communicate and engage in a way that maintains and further validates that interest. For uninterested members, the initial strategy must be to try to get them interested. One start-up superannuation fund, Spaceship, connected successfully with the values of uninterested customers and was able to generate more than 11,000 pre-registered customers prior to launching the fund (pun intended!).[27]

Most of us are familiar with the success of the global coffeehouse Starbucks. Part of their success lies in their understanding of their customer *groups* – not just numbers and segments, but groups of people differentiated by their values and behaviours.[28] One of their groups is called 'Hard-Core Loyals', which probably doesn't need much explaining! What's important is that a Hard-Core Loyal could be a 7-figure-a-year Wall Street banker who comes in on their way to work every morning, or a taxi driver in Bukit Mertajam, Malaysia who simply cannot stay away from the Starbucks at Icon City. It's not the demographics that are important – it's the behaviour.

Starbucks also know they have a large base of customers that value enjoying a coffee in a relaxed, friendly atmosphere. Some customers may use the store as a place to meet with friends or relatives for a chat, others a place to work. They understand that to deliver value to these groups of customers based on their values and behaviours, they need to make sure the coffee and food is good, the service friendly, and the environment pleasant. But what about those Hard-Core Loyals? You definitely can't ignore them, as they are likely to be your most strident advocates. A key part of the strategy must be to both value and grow this group – to retain all of the current members, while also adding new members to the group. Starbucks must focus on creating additional value for those Hard-Core Loyals, as investing in this relatively small cohort will build a more profitable customer portfolio over time.

Step 2: Understand the two-way value exchange

Let's reflect back on those Diamond Customers. They were getting value from the business in a whole range of ways, many very practical and others a bit more personal, such as through their connection with the brand. The business in turn gained long tenure from these customers, making them very profitable. Additionally, these customers provided advocacy for the business. To me this is the classic two-way exchange of value, where both parties in the relationship benefit.

Some customers endeavour to get more value than they return. Take, for example, those price-focused customers from the building supplies company. These customers were seeking deals and bargains. They would often pitch different suppliers against each other to get a better deal. For the business they were low-margin, high-maintenance customers, and what word of mouth would they provide? Probably nothing, except maybe bragging rights on the deals they had extracted. Value in this context is tipped too far towards the customer. For the long-term relationship to work, there has to be a fair and mutual exchange of value.

Likewise, some businesses like to get more from their customers than they return. Big banks are often in the negative-word-of-mouth spotlight because their customers feel the fees (for just about everything) are way out of control and only about improving bank profits, rather than providing value-adding services for the customer. They're left feeling resentful, which is a feeling that resonates with value. If an alternative appears that represents better alignment with their values, the customer will likely leave. But worse than that, when a customer perceives that a business gets more out of the relationship than they should, they will complain to anyone who will listen.

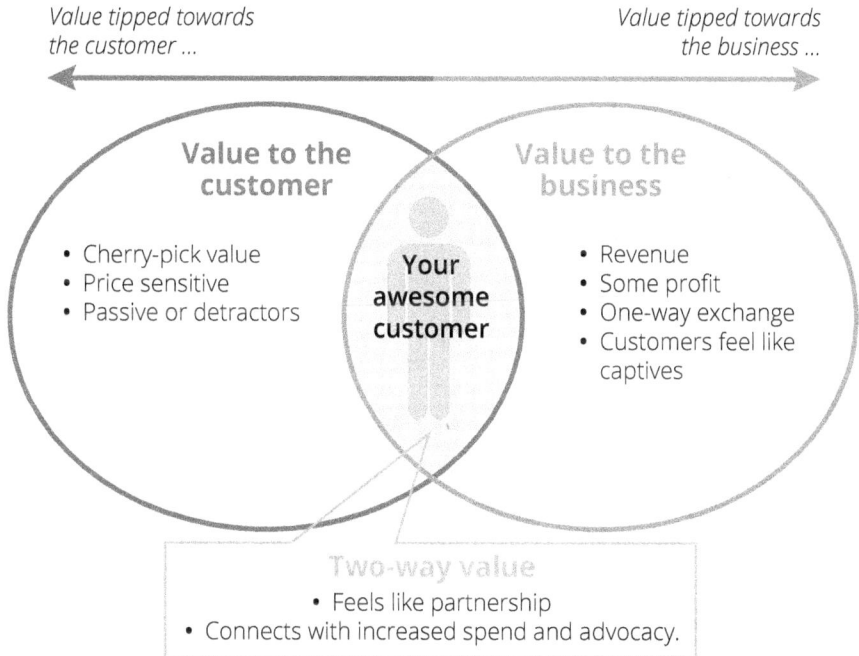

Value tipped towards the customer ...   *Value tipped towards the business ...*

Value to the customer

- Cherry-pick value
- Price sensitive
- Passive or detractors

Your awesome customer

Value to the business

- Revenue
- Some profit
- One-way exchange
- Customers feel like captives

Two-way value
- Feels like partnership
- Connects with increased spend and advocacy.

When value is tipped more towards the customer, the business doesn't receive the value it deserves for the products and services provided. A lot of retailers rely on discounts and sales to get customers into the store (physical or online) hoping that, while the customer is there, they will also buy some undiscounted products. However, some customers will cherry-pick the value for themselves, only buying the specials and representing very little value to the retailer – possibly even negative value, given the cost to serve. Interestingly, when customers are in this zone they *still* tend not to provide positive word of mouth, because they don't feel like they're in a relationship with the business. They are simply transacting. They're passive customers, or possibly even detractors if they encourage others to treat the business the same way.

The sweet spot is where the customer gets the value the business delivers, and the business in turn receives a fair price and advocacy from the customer. Customers value the solutions and services the business provides. And the business has profitable promoters in its customer portfolio.

To understand this idea of the two-way value exchange more deeply, let's look into how customers define value. Then, in the next chapter, we'll consider in detail how businesses can assess value.

How customers define value

It is commonly recognised that most salespeople cannot articulate value for their customers. They're trapped in the mindset of only noticing the value they give, rather than the value the customer receives. A subtle difference, but an all-important one! This leads them to talk more about the features of their offerings than the actual benefits to the customer. It is the same with most businesses – there is way too much focus on the products.

Customers define value very differently – differently to organisations, differently to salespeople, and differently to each other. And if we hope to be able to offer value to them, we need to understand those different definitions.[29]

I often see value described like this: 'An accountant saves the customer $5000 in tax and only charges $2000, therefore the value for the customer is $3000.' Or 'The RRP on this product is $45, but you pay $27, therefore you save $18.'

These equations are far too generic and simplistic. In fact, they miss the point completely. Value is not just about dollars. As we've already noted, customers buy based on emotions. It seems obvious, then, that these emotions are a key part of the value they're getting out of the product and service experience. The rational part of value is not the full story. Perceived value is just as important.

So what is it the customer is looking for? Well, it basically comes down to three aspects.

The customer wants to achieve a goal

When we start to think of the sources of value for our customers, we tend to think first of the product itself or the service delivered. Or maybe we mention physical resources, such as a shop or restaurant. If challenged, we might move into ideas of service excellence (think high-end department stores) or consistency and attention to detail (like McDonald's).

However, customers define value in very different terms. Customers tend to think of value in terms of goals or results. That is, the outcome they are seeking. Customers seeking to buy a new home are often regaled with the details of a loan and mortgage. But what if a finance broker came along who actually talked about their ability to collaborate with solicitors and settle on the home on their behalf? Now that would get the customer's attention. Customers don't really want 'a mortgage'. They want to get into their new home with the least hassle possible. And that is rarely communicated.

Similarly, when someone goes to sell a house, the real estate agent will often talk at length about the marketing package – signage, internet listings, sole agency agreements, etc. This customer does not want 'a marketing package with a lock-in agreement'. They just want their house sold at a fair price! That is the goal or result they seek.

The customer wants a positive experience

The customer's overall perception of value is dominated not only by the outcome itself, but also by their end-to-end experience during delivery of the outcome. So, to return to the earlier example of buying a new home, if the finance company made the process of buying the home a complete hassle, the customer would be unlikely to promote the finance business despite having achieved their goal. It's more likely they would be a detractor, providing negative word of mouth freely.

The customer wants a sense of community

Finally, customers can define value based on the feeling and benefits they get from belonging to a community.[30] The managers of musicians and sporting teams have known this for quite a while, and the investment fans make into merchandise is quite extraordinary. However, it goes a step further. The most successful brands have built or inspired such a deep sense of community in their fans that it has become a marker of identity. Fans display their affiliation with their favourite artists by sporting logos and brand names on their clothes, coffee cups, and even guitars. Harley Davidson Motor Company survived to become a leading global brand despite America's complete lack of reputation for motorcycle manufacturing. How? Primarily thanks to their community of 'Hogs' (Harley Owners Group) – people that love to wear the brand logo, attend events, and advocate loudly for the brand.

Customers define the value they get based on the results or goals they realise. This is why we start with understanding what customers value. We then add to this by optimising the experience they have in realising these goals, and, if possible, create some sense of value in community. Let go of the outdated idea that customers define value in terms of features and advantages of products or services. Yes, they need to know what a product does. But that's not the part that makes them into a profitable promoter.

———

We can often get a better handle on customer perception of value by seeing value as a function of the benefits received over the sacrifices made in getting the benefits.

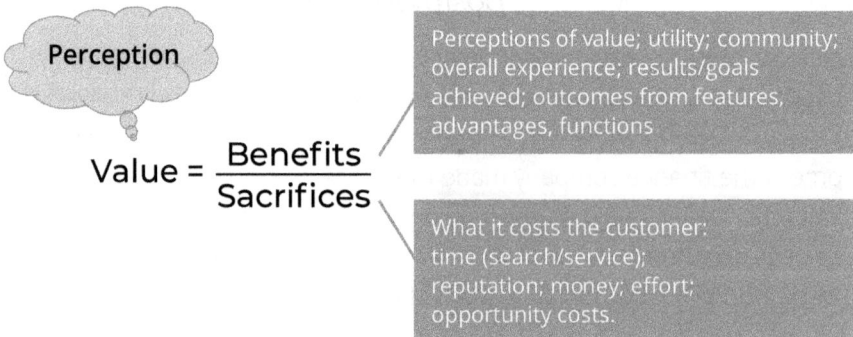

Perception

Perceptions of value; utility; community; overall experience; results/goals achieved; outcomes from features, advantages, functions

$$Value = \frac{Benefits}{Sacrifices}$$

What it costs the customer: time (search/service); reputation; money; effort; opportunity costs.

The products and services we deliver have functions and features that enable customers to achieve things, however small or large, which then leads to realisation of goals, results, and outcomes – that is, value for the customer. As we mentioned above, value for the customer also lies in how these goals are achieved. Was it complicated, did it take a lot of effort and hassle, or was it easy? This is value from experience. Then there is the actual monetary cost, combined with the time and effort the customer has put in. Compared against the benefits, does it represent value for the customer? The combination of all these factors determines the customer's overall perception of value. And it is a *perception*. It may not match your reality, but it is a very persistent reality for them.

The Customer Value Map

A useful way to examine customer value in detail is to use a Customer Value Map. To see how this works, let's return to the example of a residential seller (customer) using the services of a real-estate agent.

The Customer Value Map identifies the features, advantages, and functions that the customer receives from the business, in this case the real-estate agent. From these functions the customer (hopefully) realises their goals, results, and outcomes. But the sum total of perceived benefits is not complete without a consideration of the overall experience. The timeline, price, and general enjoyment of the experience also needs to be taken into account. Just as we saw in the previous diagram, the customer's overall perception of value is a balance between the benefits they have realised and the costs/sacrifices they have experienced.

———

As a side note, mapping out how your customers experience value like this can make something that seems intangible very real and measurable. For example, asking residential sellers to complete a simple survey upon completion of the sale and asking questions based on the four feeders into perceived benefits will provide a measure of your customers' perceptions, likewise for costs and sacrifices. You could even ask customers to rate which of the four feeders is most and least important. From this data you'll gain genuine insights into what your customers value.

Customer value map
Customer group: Residential sellers (for real estate agent)

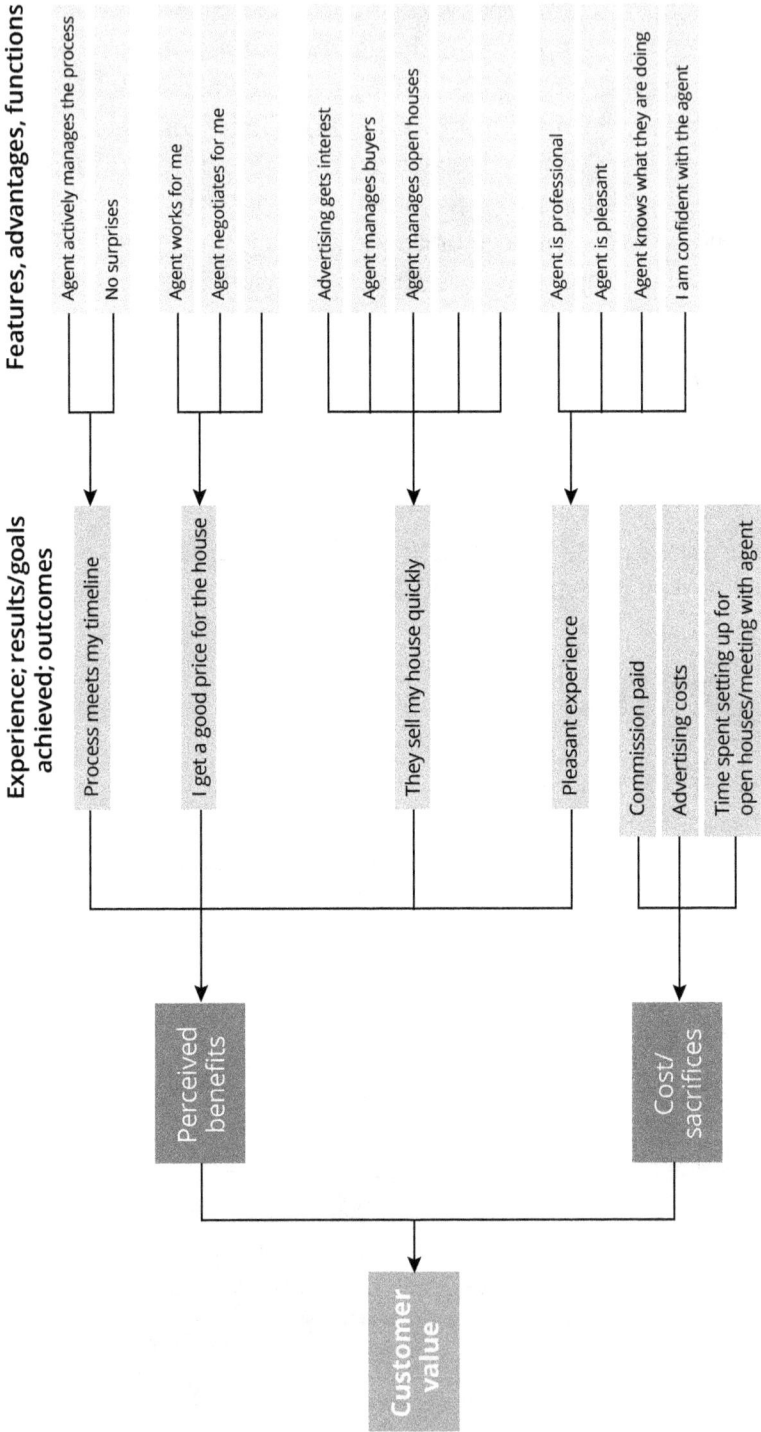

Features, advantages, functions

- Agent actively manages the process
- No surprises
- Agent works for me
- Agent negotiates for me
- Advertising gets interest
- Agent manages buyers
- Agent manages open houses
- Agent is professional
- Agent is pleasant
- Agent knows what they are doing
- I am confident with the agent

Experience; results/goals achieved; outcomes

- Process meets my timeline
- I get a good price for the house
- They sell my house quickly
- Pleasant experience

- Commission paid
- Advertising costs
- Time spent setting up for open houses/meeting with agent

Perceived benefits

Cost/ sacrifices

Customer value

The real-estate example above is fairly straightforward, but understanding the two-way value exchange can get a little more complex in some cases. What happens when you provide a service to multiple customer groups with different needs? What if providing maximum value for one customer group means negatively impacting the value provided for another? How do you balance these needs?

Quest Community Newspapers is a subsidiary of News Corp Australia located in Bowen Hills, Queensland.[31] Quest provides a free weekly community newspaper with articles about what's going on in the community – and, of course, advertising. This means that for each free community newspaper, Quest have two main customer groups: Readers and Advertisers.

For Quest, the Advertiser customer group would have subgroups such as large retailers, tradespeople, and government agencies. Each subgroup would have similar needs – to reach a specific audience and send clear messages to target groups, with the overall goal to increase sales or simply communicate with their target audience.

The Reader customer group would also have a few subgroups, represented as personas. These people are looking for various aspects of value from the newspaper – feeling engaged with the community, knowing what's going on, and seeing where the bargains are. However, if Quest increases the amount of advertising to a point that the content Readers are looking for is hard to find or just not there, then Readers disengage and Advertisers no longer have an audience.

Quest needs to balance the value between these two customer groups. Too much advertising space reduces value for Readers, which means Advertisers lose their audience. Value needs to be created for both groups. One of the ways that Quest do this very nicely is through an annual reader survey. Readers willingly complete a detailed survey on the promise that Quest will publish the results in the newspaper. Readers get to see a public summary of their community profile – who's around them, what the values of their community are, any changes in demographics – but so do Advertisers. This valuable information about Readers allows Quest to attract premium pricing from Advertisers wanting to engage with a specific Reader group. Quest also gets an opportunity to reassess the alignment between specific Reader personas and the individuals within those subgroups.

Summary

The process of developing a Customer Strategy begins with identifying customer groups. This needn't be overwhelming. Just start with whatever comes to mind, and work from there. What differentiates these groups? What are their attributes? What is their potential spend? How do they buy, spend, and promote? What do they value, and how do they define that value?

Next, it's a matter of working out what value you can offer to each customer group, and what value they can offer in return. The optimal two-way exchange of value occurs when the customer gets the best possible value from the business, and the customer reciprocates that value both financially and in the form of advocacy. Customers define value based on three main things: whether they achieve their desired goal, the experience they have in realising that goal, and whether the experience offers a sense of community.

———

Templates available for this chapter:

1. Identifying Customer Groups Template
2. Customer Value Map Template
3. How your Customer Defines Value Template

CHAPTER SIX

VALUE FOR THE BUSINESS FROM CUSTOMERS

In this chapter, we'll dive deep into the value customers can provide to the business. This discussion will focus in on two primary areas: financial value, and word of mouth.

Customer advocacy

Positive word of mouth from customers has always been important to business, but today its impact is on steroids. In the late 1990s, eBay and others pioneered the implementation of customer feedback into online selling platforms. This meant that customers could provide feedback on sellers, their service, and their products. Customer feedback on this scale was a game changer. Now, these kinds of online reviews permeate every industry. Customers turn to reviews before making almost any decision, from local restaurants to international hotels, mobile phones to passenger flights. It is an undeniable fact that the amount of positive or negative word of mouth received from customers is of significant importance for any type of business or organisation today.

In the last century many organisations used to ask their customers, quite simply, how 'satisfied' they were. But we discovered in the 1990s that satisfaction wasn't a predictor of future behaviour. In financial services (and other industries), we were finding that customers would say they were satisfied – and then leave us. In other words, it appeared that satisfaction was something the customer felt in the moment (or two), but it didn't mean they would repurchase, or even provide positive word of mouth. Using 'customer satisfaction' measures was, it turned out, like looking into a rear-vision mirror when you're trying to figure out where you're going. So how *could* businesses figure out what their customers were going to do? This was the problem Fred Reichheld applied himself to.

Reichheld always knew that customer loyalty was critically important, and published his ideas for the first time in *The Loyalty Effect* in 1996.[32] It was around this time that 'loyalty programs' really took off. Unfortunately, most organisations turned the idea of loyalty into a transactional concept. They thought they were in a relationship with the customer, while the customer was really just looking for better value. But even as Reichheld encouraged businesses to figure out what customer loyalty meant for them, he knew it was still too vague a concept to predict future customer behaviour, and was lacking as a tool for improving performance. And so he persisted, partnering with Bain and Co to find a way to predict customer behaviour. They tested their ideas and published their findings in *The Ultimate Question*.[33] The answer? What we know today as the Net Promoter Score.

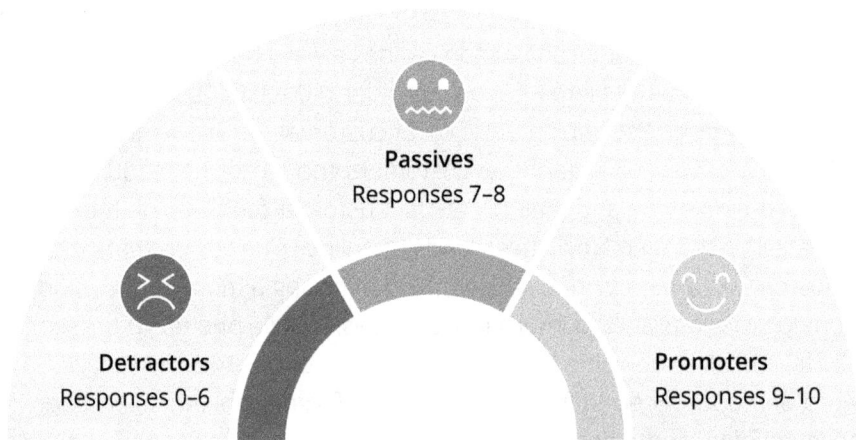

Passives
Responses 7–8

Detractors
Responses 0–6

Promoters
Responses 9–10

The Net Promoter Score (NPS) is determined based on customer responses to a simple question: 'How likely are you to recommend [insert business/service/product] to your friends, family and colleagues?' The NPS is equal to the percentage of customers that score you 9 or 10 (we call these people 'promoters') minus the percentage of customers that score you 0–6 ('detractors'). For example, imagine you ask 100 customers the question. If 25 people give you a 9 or 10 (promoters), 55 give you a 7 or 8 (passives); and 20 score you somewhere between 0 and 6 ('detractors'), your NPS is 5 (25 minus 20).

Bain and Reichheld tested and researched this 'ultimate question' extensively and proved that it does in fact predict the future behaviour of a customer – primarily, their inclination to provide word or mouth. Someone giving a service provider 9 or 10 would indeed be highly likely to provide positive word of mouth for that business. Those scoring 0 to 6, not so much. In fact, these people are likely to tell others not to have anything to do with you, and probably have a couple of poor service stories they enjoy telling. 'Passives', those people that score 7 or 8, are not likely to recommend or give negative word of mouth.

So, to continue with the example above, what exactly does an NPS of 5 mean? Well, it tells you that right now there are slightly more people in the market speaking well of you than there are 'bagging' you. This is a good thing! However, as with all measures, we should track it over time to get a more useful sense of our place in the market.

Net promotor score (monthly)

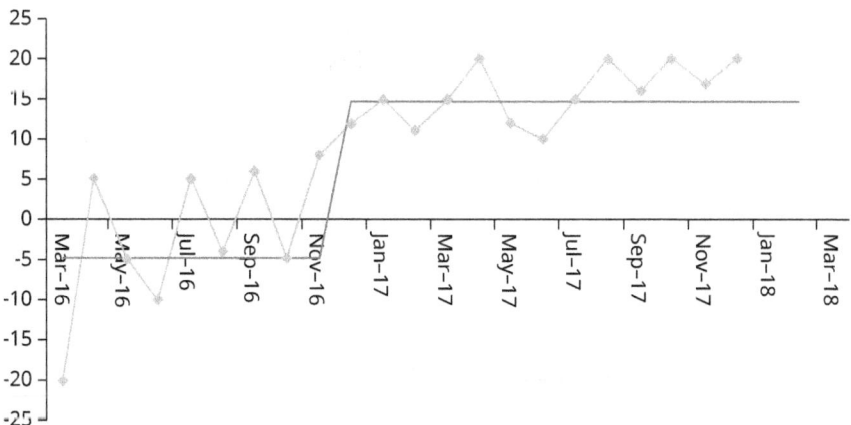

The above chart depicts almost two years of monthly NPS values. We can see that this organisation has improved its NPS from a monthly average of –5 to around 15, which is a great improvement.[34]

Having more people in your marketplace saying positive things and recommending people to come to you is an awesome value for any organisation. It's as if your customers are your own marketing. Even better, if you have defined your awesome customers and they are the customers that are recommending others join you, then you will more than likely be growing that portion of your customer portfolio. And that's where the gold is for businesses.

The trick with NPS is that it's not really about the value itself. It's more about what it means within your customer ecosystem. What other choices are available to them? For example, if you are in financial services and your NPS is –2 (the current average for financial services in Australia), then setting a goal to get to 20 might mean investing more than you need to. Even increasing your NPS to 5 means you are probably better than the alternatives available to your customers – and it is your customers saying this!

When it comes to your customer portfolio, measuring NPS is much better done at a customer-group level. The average NPS value of the whole customer portfolio does not tell you anything actionable. It tells you nothing about the progress you are making on your Customer Strategy. The goal is to increase the NPS within your chosen customer groups.

The value to the business from customers here is their positive word of mouth. This isn't just free advertising – it's better, because people make decisions emotionally. If someone recommends your services or product to a friend, that friend is predisposed to give you the chance to deserve that recommendation. When you deliver on this, you will probably have won another advocate.

Depending on your business and offerings, the flow-on effects of having more promoters than detractors can be:

- reduced costs to acquire new customers (potentially reducing marketing costs)
- improved customer retention

- increased product uptake, cross-selling, and up-sales (customers are more likely to trust you and be receptive to your offers, though of course this still need to add value for them)
- reduced customer price sensitivity.

All this makes for better margins, which leads to:

- improved cost-to-income ratios, and ultimately
- improved customer lifetime value, which we will discuss now.

Customer lifetime value

The calculation of customer lifetime value (CLV) takes into consideration the value of your customers over time – not just the initial purchase, but potential repeat purchases, subscriptions, and renewals. It's the financial value of the customer for the whole time they are with you.

As with all calculations going into the future, there are assumptions and limitations. The main assumptions here are that the costs, retention rates, and margins remain constant over time. This is why I refer to customer lifetime value as eCLV – *estimated* customer lifetime value. Some organisations have the data and resources to use CLV to great effect. But most seem to get bogged down in trying to get the calculations perfect. They get hung up on the inaccuracy of CLV and allow themselves to devolve into uncertainty and no action. Don't fall into this trap. CLV is just an *estimate* – one that can help you make more informed decisions when it comes to your customers.

My aim here is to provide you with an approach to unlock insights into your customer portfolio and grow your customer base profitably.

Here's the formula:

$$CLV = m \left(\frac{r}{1 + i - r} \right)$$

Where:
m = margin
r = retention rate
i = cash discount rate

— from Gupta and Lehman (2005)[35]

Don't panic! It's actually simpler than it looks. Basically, CLV takes the margin (*m*) for a particular customer group and multiplies it by a factor (the part in brackets). This factor depends on the retention rate (*r*) of that particular customer group, and the cash discount rate (*i*).

The cash discount rate (*i*) is a way of taking into account the fact that a dollar today is worth much more than a dollar next year, or even ten years from now. The cash discount rate is also used in the NPV (net present value) method of assessing investments to 'discount' the future value of a dollar to today's rate. We do the exact same thing when we calculate CLV, which is why it's known as a 'discounted cash flow method'.

So the three pieces of data you need to have – or at least estimate – for each calculation are:

- the margin for a representative customer of the customer group (income less cost),
- the retention rate of the customer group, and
- the cash discount rate (check this with your accountant or finance people).

To simplify things, we can translate the expression inside the brackets of the above formula into a table that gives us the multiplier for the margin under different conditions (different retention rates and cash discount rates).

Margin Multiplier

		Interest rate / Discount rate / Cost of capital					
		4%	6%	8%	10%	12%	14%	16%
Rentention rate	50%	0.93	0.89	0.86	0.83	0.81	0.78	0.76
	60%	1.36	1.30	1.25	1.20	1.15	1.11	1.07
	70%	2.06	1.94	1.84	1.75	1.67	1.59	1.52
	80%	3.33	3.08	2.86	2.67	2.50	2.35	2.22
	90%	6.43	5.63	5.00	4.50	4.09	3.75	3.46
	100%	10.56	8.64	7.31	6.33	5.59	5.00	4.52

Now for some examples.

Let's say a subscription to the premium version of LinkedIn is priced at $48 per month. Assume the cost of acquisition is $35, and the ongoing cost of the service is $4 per month. Total cost to the organisation for the first year is therefore $83 (cost of acquisition plus service cost for the year); however, ongoing years should incur only the service cost of $48 ($4 x 12 months). Let's say the cost of capital is 8% per annum, and premium subscribers have a retention rate of 90% per annum.

Revenue per customer is $48 x 12 = $576 for the first year (and subsequent years). The margin, then, is $83 less: $493. Multiplying the margin by the multiplier (from the table above, for 8% interest rate and 90% retention) gives us: $493 x 5 = $2,465.

Consider the following questions:

- How much would you invest in customer engagement activity to add one of these customers to your portfolio?
- If retention of these customers went up to 95%, the eCLV would be $3,603.83. How much would you invest into understanding how to retain more of these customers?

Now let's recall again the financial services group we looked at earlier. The average profit contribution per customer was $687, and the average retention was about 80%. Using 8% cost of capital again, the eCLV for the average customer is: $687 x 2.86 = $1,687.

But what about those Diamond Customers in among the portfolio? Their annual profit contribution was $2,767. The retention rate was as high as 99% for many of those customers, but let's be conservative and round down the retention rate down to 95%. Again using 8% cost of capital, the eCLV for those customers is: $2,767 x 7.31 = $20,227.

- How much effort and investment would you put into ensuring that the Diamond Customers are the customer group that grows?

This example demonstrates the flaw in averages.[36] There is no such thing, really, as an average customer, but we can have *representative* customers and specific customer groups. Our task is to understand these various groups, the different value they represent to the business, and why.

Step 3: Create customer intent

Now that we have defined our customers groups, and figured out (or at least estimated) the value these customers are getting from us and the value they reciprocate, we should be much closer to knowing which customers we want to grow. These are the ones that we want to form a larger portion of our customer portfolio. Sure, this process might involve a little trial and error, but until we develop a hypothesis and test it, we won't learn. In this step of creating the Customer Strategy, we will determine the intent we want to have with each group.

The table opposite describes the seven core intents an organisation may have with a customer group and the expected outcomes or results.[37] The idea or challenge is to select only one or two intents for each customer group. This will give your Customer Strategy focus and clarity.

So how do we apply this process to create our Customer Strategy? Let's look at how it applies to a few of the examples we've been looking at.

Remember those Hard-Core Loyals from Starbucks? You want more of these customers in your portfolio, as they fulfil their half of the two-way value exchange by being great customers and providing advocacy. Therefore, the strategy for this group is to *Grow*. So where will these new Hard-Core Loyals come from? Some may be added directly to the portfolio, if the company's value proposition resonates with their goal. Others may come from other existing customer groups. Ask yourself: Who are the existing customers most likely to become Hard-Core Loyals? Once you identify this customer group, your challenge is to *Enhance* the relationship and add value for those customers so that they become Hard-Core Loyals. This is similar to the approach taken with the Diamond Customers in Chapter 2.

Consider now those price-focused customers for the B2B supplier. The intent for those customers should be *Maintain* the relationship. These

Intent	Description	Expected result
Grow	Acquire more of these types of customers.	Increased portion of the customer portfolio
Protect the relationship	Apply proactive retention approaches to engage with these strategically important (value/leverage) customers, with the net effect of not losing any customers.	These customers are retained
Maintain the relationship	Maintain a transactional relationship with these customers; provide service with the view of minimal cost and provision of basic needs.	Many of these customers may be retained Cost to serve reduced
Re-engineer the relationship	Change the way these customers interact with us, or how they behave in the environment. Consider reducing the cost to serve these customers, and therefore changing the way the relationship works.	Portion of the customer portfolio grows Cost to serve reduces
Enhance the relationship	Change customer behaviour similarly to 'Re-engineer', but with a focus on delivering additional value to the customer.	Retain the customers that accept higher value
Win back	Identify customers of value that have been lost and develop tactics to win them back.	Re-engage with these customers
End the relationship	Cut these customers off. These customers represent no value to the organisation. This is where we can see no other alternative to Maintain, Re-engineer or Enhance the relationship.	These customers are dropped from the portfolio

customers don't really value service or a partnership relationship, so the optimal thing to do is simply transact with these customers. Don't give any additional time or effort to doing deals or bargaining. To do this would be to waste your resources and reduce your margin. Determine instead to maintain this relationship through a basic, transactional service approach. There may be a subset of these customers that you might be able to migrate towards a service focus using a *Re-engineer* intent, where you intend to change the way you interact with them and influence their perception of the value from your service.

Finally, the high-usage subscribers to the free version of LinkedIn would most likely be targeted for *Re-engineer* or *Enhance*, by making offers to upgrade to the premium version of LinkedIn.

Tips for implementing the Customer Strategy

As we saw in Chapter 5, developing your Customer Strategy is an iterative process that starts with simply writing down the first customer groups that spring to mind and searching for the behavioural differentiators within those groups. We then seek to understand the value each group seeks, and the value each group provides back to the organisation through eCLV or advocacy.

Now take a fresh look at your customer groups. Does knowing more about the two-way value exchange change your perspective of the groups you have your customers in? We often use deductive and inductive reasoning and logic to forms these groups, but I have often found abductive logic very useful. Abductive reasoning has us looking at the customers that often don't fit, or a group that seems out of place.[38] Often those unusual customers can be your 'diamonds in the rough'.

I promise you, this iterative, a back-and-forth approach to defining your customer groups *is* effective. Do not focus on getting it perfect. But once you have a basic outline, narrow the focus by selecting one, or maybe two, 'intents' for each customer group. Your customer groups, your understanding of two-way value, and the intent you have chosen for each group now forms your Customer Strategy. In the next chapter we'll look into how we can articulate our value propositions for each group.

Summary

We've seen that the value that a particular customer (being part of a specific customer group) brings to an organisation is twofold:

- advocacy – the level of positive word of mouth and recommendations the customer provides for you, and

- eCLV – the customer's (estimated) lifetime financial value, derived from the margin and retention rate of the representative customer and discounted for future values.

With an understanding of your customer groups and the two-way value exchange, you are now in a position to define the customer intent for each group. Depending on the nature and extent of the two-way value exchange, you will decide whether to *Grow*, *Protect*, *Maintain*, *Re-engineer*, *Enhance*, *Win Back*, or *End* the relationship with each customer group.

At this point, you have finally identified your awesome customers – the group that offers optimal value exchange, and that you are determined to *Grow*. These customers could be:

- a subset of your total available market (where other customer groups offer much less value), such as the partnership-focused customers in the building supplies example;

- created or maintained with a relationship configuration that delivers two-way value, and better value than other configurations, as in the case of the Diamond Customers;

- from multiple customer groups that deliver better overall value to the business when they are supported in balance, as we saw in the case of Quest; or

- Potentially a wide range of other configurations, depending on your specific context.

————

Templates available for this chapter:

1. The NPS Calculation Template

2. eCLV Calculation Template

3. Intent with a Customer Group Template

CHAPTER SEVEN
CUSTOMER VALUE PROPOSITIONS

In Phase 1 of designing the business with a view to deliberately creating the customer portfolio, the key output from our efforts was the development of our overarching Customer Strategy. This is the documented articulation of who our customer groups are, the two-way value exchange between the customer group and the business, and the chosen intent with each customer group. We've seen that the Customer Strategy is iterative. It is not about perfection, but about being practical. Therefore, we implement our first version of the Customer Strategy knowing that we will continue to learn more as we go, and that our Customer Strategy will continue to be refined and redefined.

But before we get into implementation, we need to define how we communicate value for our various customer groups. We must be clear and precise in our messaging. Our customers' world is very noisy, so we must know how to communicate value in a way that resonates with the specific customer groups we have chosen to grow. This will ensure we build the customer portfolio we need.

Moving into Phase 2

After we have developed a detailed and clear understanding of our customer groups in our Customer Strategy, we can then (and only then) start to consider how we explain and illustrate value for our customers.

We must learn how to articulate value before we start delivering value. While this might seem obvious, most organisations don't do it. Either they have a product-centric approach (which skips the customer totally) and go about describing the features from their products, or they gloss over the Customer Strategy and jump immediately into the doing – the delivery of value. The task of creating and presenting value propositions is then delegated to sales and/or marketing teams – sometimes concurrently. This leaves the creation of our customer portfolio purely to chance.

We want to grow specific groups of customers. We want to change the way some customer relationships work. Crafting clear value propositions before we delegate action will ensure our Customer Strategy is guiding the development of the customer portfolio.

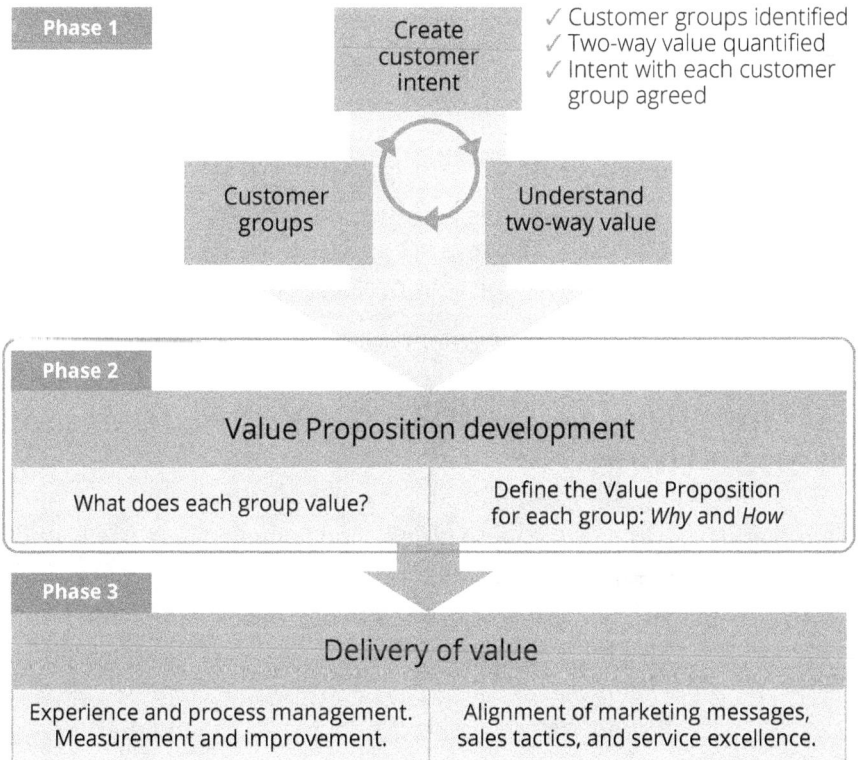

Phase 1

Create customer intent

✓ Customer groups identified
✓ Two-way value quantified
✓ Intent with each customer group agreed

Customer groups

Understand two-way value

Phase 2

Value Proposition development

What does each group value?

Define the Value Proposition for each group: *Why* and *How*

Phase 3

Delivery of value

Experience and process management. Measurement and improvement.

Alignment of marketing messages, sales tactics, and service excellence.

The value propositions you develop must resonate with each customer group. What is it that each customer group values? How do they define the results or goals they are trying to achieve? What overall experience are they anticipating? Will they gain any value from being part of a community? Knowing the answers to these questions will allow us to communicate more meaningfully the value we can deliver for the customer. We can more easily articulate the two-way value exchange when we understand it. However, we know that our customers make decisions emotionally and *then* seek to justify the decision with rationale. In other words, decisions originate from the emotional part of the brain, which uses not language but feelings. Our logical brain doesn't even get involved until we try articulate the decision we have made.

Therefore, when it comes to value propositions for our chosen customer groups, we need to provide an *emotional why* for the customer. Why engage with us? Why buy from us? I call this the level 1 value proposition. Next, we also need to provide rationale for the what and the how. To me, this is a level 2 value proposition. We will look more into level 1 and 2 value propositions soon, but first let's have a look at some of the common ideas and language of value propositions that are currently doing the rounds. The purpose of looking at these ideas is so that we can more fully understand what we are doing when developing meaningful value statements for our customers. By picking out the strengths and weaknesses of some common value propositions, we'll gain a better understanding of what should be considered at each level.

Frequently used ideas for value propositions

Many marketing texts define value proposition something like this: A value proposition is the explicit (and sometimes implicit) promise made by a company to its customers that it will deliver a particular set of benefits that will create value for the customer. Personally, I prefer the way Ash Maurya puts it in *Running Lean*: A unique value proposition is "why you are worth getting attention", as "selling is a conversation" and the first challenge is to get someone's attention.[39]

Other definitions abound, many specific to generic bundles of products or services. In this product-centric world, most value propositions are normally about the product or service. Or perhaps some promises from the brand itself. As we noted in the previous chapter, these are not the things our customers actually value! Regardless of which level the value proposition is at, it still needs to resonate with your specific chosen customer groups – firstly at an emotional level, and secondly with rationale.

So let's have a look at some of the common value proposition approaches used in the market.

USPs and VPs

Unique selling propositions (USPs), or unique selling points, have been used (and probably still are) to convince customers to make a buying decisions. I feel that USPs are often confused with value propositions. In the past, marketing and selling organisations believed that customers bought logically. Therefore, if you came up with a solid rational statement there would be no reason for the customer not to buy. For example, in the last century people selling sets of encyclopaedias would use a USP that compared the value of your child's education to the price of a cup of coffee (daily for a few months as you paid off the set of books). Surely a no-brainer!

British retailer Tesco, which offers services like home deliveries and online ordering, uses the tagline 'Every little helps', supported by the statement 'Never pay more for your branded shop.' Avis car rental proposes that 'We try harder.' And we all know that 'The burgers are better at Hungry Jacks.' These statements might be advertising slogans – and perhaps overarching value propositions – but they are based in a comparison to alternatives available to the customer. Compare this to the world's largest online retailer Amazon, which just says, 'Everything from A to Z.'

Other USPs might come in the form of service promises. Domino's pizza, for example, for many years promised to deliver your pizza within '30 minutes or it's free.' Disney famously claim to 'create happiness through magical experiences', and calls Disneyland 'The happiest place on earth.' When it comes to products, Levi's claim that 'Quality never goes out of style', and BMW promise the 'ultimate driving machine'. But making these overarching promises isn't enough. The lower-level statements of value need to create a framework that is meaningful for the customer.

In a 2006 article in the *Harvard Business Review*, three professors from the USA and the Netherlands presented research into how businesses communicate value to their customers.[40] They divided the value propositions used into three categories. The 'all benefits' value proposition presents the prospective customer with all the reasons why they should by from the selling business. The second type of value proposition identifies 'all favourable points of difference a market offering has relative to the next best alternative' – all the reasons why the customer should buy from you as opposed to someone else – and in doing so makes an assumption of value. The third value proposition with, 'resonating focus', describes only the couple of points of difference that deliver the greatest value for the prospective customer, compared to alternatives.

These types of value propositions are still prolific. However, research by CEB published in *The Challenger Sales* (2011) claims that general information businesses can find on the internet does not create differentiating value propositions.[41] For example, TechnologyOne is a business that provides enterprise systems for large organisations. One of its chosen customer groups is Local Government (Councils). TechnologyOne attempts to differentiate itself from other providers by claiming that its '[c]ommitment to an enterprise vision for local governments enables authorities to reduce costs, improve efficiencies and streamline processes through end-to-end management of council operations.'[42] This statement is generic. The benefits claimed are generic. In fact, any other provider would claim exactly the same. Instead, TechnologyOne should present key insights – derived from the benefits – into how they are creating value for the customer. They should surprise customers with their unique approach to genuine value creation.

In an era where the customer has more information available to them than ever in history, and where customers are resistant to sales pitches, we need to find a way for our messages to deeply resonate with our chosen customers. Let's look at a couple of current approaches.

Jobs theory

The ideas behind 'Jobs to be done', or 'Jobs theory', came to Professor Clayton Christensen of Harvard Business School while working with McDonalds to try to sell more milkshakes. He began asking customers, 'Why buy a milkshake?' They discovered that most of their milkshakes were sold at the drive-through in the mornings. Customers were looking for something to put in their stomachs – and something to do – while on their commute. Christensen and his team of researchers determined that this was the *job* the customer wanted to do. Some customers used bananas or doughnuts for this job, but the milkshake was the preferred option. To sell more milkshakes, McDonald's did not have to introduce new flavours or price promotions. They just had to find ways to trigger customers to want a milkshake as company for their commute.

Christensen says that we are far better off to start by understanding the job the customer is trying to do, and then test what things the customer can *hire* to get that job done.[43] He says that by understanding what causes the customer to *hire* a particular product or service to get a job done, we will discover new products or services to offer these customers.

'Jobs to be done' is therefore really about helping product-focused people and businesses to stop focusing on the solution and start focusing on what the customer is trying to achieve – which is a good start! When you shift your focus like this, you can develop value propositions that are about the *job* and the *hire*. A perfect example of successfully encouraging customers to *hire* a service is demonstrated by (again!) those well-known golden arches. Many years ago, McDonald's realised that having a children's birthday party at home was often traumatic, chaotic, and messy for the parents. So they allowed parents to hire a room and staff to do it for them. And they sold a lot of cheeseburgers, fries, and drinks while they were at it!

Value Proposition Canvas

Swiss business consultant and theorist Alexander Ostewalder initiated and co-developed the Business Model Canvas, which has gained popularity in recent times.[44] Within their model they use a Value Proposition Canvas (VPC). This is about matching your product with what your customer is trying to achieve. On the customer side of the VPC, they advocate looking at the 'jobs' the customer is trying to do (similar to jobs theory), which can be functional, social, or emotional. Customers achieve gains from fulfilling the jobs they have to do. They also experience pains, fears, frustrations, and obstacles in the process. As we saw with the McDonald's example, a milkshake alleviated two customer pains: that empty feeling in their stomach, and the boredom of the commute. The basic idea behind the VPC is that you examine the features of your products and services and match them with customer gains and pains. This then becomes the basis for communicating value to the customer.

The VPC approach to value propositions targets the job the customer is trying to get done, reducing the associated pains and maximising the gains. While the VPC is still a product-centric approach, it does take into account the perspectives of the customer, which is a good thing. Using the VPC over time with a focus of reducing pains and improving gains could potentially produce benefits for the customer, with flow-on benefits to the value of the customer portfolio. However, it's not perfect. The value propositions we really want are the ones that will resonate with the customers we are sure will become profitable promoters of what we do.

So what should we do? How do we move away from these mainly product-based value propositions to find ones that really connect with the customers we want?

Level 1 value proposition development

We need something better. The challenge with the previous ideas is that they are mainly based on selling. They aim to convince and persuade, not to engage with the *human being* – who happens to be within your chosen customer group and who you are pretty sure will get value from what you do. We know today's customers are extremely sales resistant – use anything that sounds like or feels like selling, and resistance levels automatically rise. So we need to offer a value proposition that engages with the customer. Let's illustrate this using Simon Sinek's example from his famous TED talk *How Great Leaders Inspire Action*:[45]

> If Apple were like everyone else, a marketing message from them might sound like this: 'We make great computers. They're beautifully designed, simple to use and user friendly. Want to buy one?'
>
> Here's how Apple actually communicates: 'Everything we do, we believe in challenging the status quo. We believe in thinking differently. The way we challenge the status quo is by making our products beautifully designed, simple to use and user friendly. We just happen to make great computers. Want to buy one?'

The second statement is about what the business believes and the way they want to change the world. That's *why* they exist. Businesses need to be able to articulate their why. Why is it that this customer should engage with you? What common ground and beliefs do you share? What do you stand for, and can the customer engage with this? How are you changing the world?

There are many organisations that sell their products based on establishing a values-based connection with their customers. Organisations often demonstrate that their products are good for the environment (or at least better than others), thereby connecting with customers who value protecting the earth. Others sell products that are not tested on animals or, even better, take the position of being *against* animal testing, and therefore connect with customers on moral grounds.

Australian make-up producer Nude by Nature used two core value propositions to attract a large customer base. The first VP was: '100% naturally derived with no synthetics', and the second was 'cruelty free'.[46] These two VPs were a big factor in helping Nude by Nature become 'Australia's Number 1 Mineral Make-Up'. Through research into their customer portfolio, they discovered that over time they had actually fostered two distinct customer groups. One group bought the products because they were naturally derived mineral products with no synthetics. The second group engaged with the brand based on their position of being cruelty free, with absolutely no form of animal testing or exploitation.

Nude by Nature realised that these two broad groups had engaged with the brand for different reasons, yet the messaging they were receiving was identical, supporting both value propositions. Nude by Nature decided to separate the whole portfolio of customers into these two groups and provide communications specific to the reason they had engaged. This change in communication pushed Nude by Nature's NPS (Net Promoter Score) from the high 30's up to 71! The level of advocacy from their customer portfolio increased significantly when they changed their messaging to better resonate with the reason *why* the customer had initially engaged with them.

Developing a level 1 value proposition

It's all well and good to talk about the benefits of a level 1 value proposition. But how do we actually go about developing our own? This is an important question. Many companies get stuck here and take a shortcut, diving into the product propositions without first articulating why a customer should even consider engaging with them.

A couple of years ago I worked with a small business that had developed a software package for contractors such as swimming pool installers, building renovators, and residential or small commercial builders. The business had been bought out by a retired builder, Kev, who really believed in the product. Kev and I had developed our Customer Strategy and were now at the value proposition stage. Kev and his team were fantastic at describing all the system's bells and whistles and *how* everyone should be using it. But there was no *why* for a customer to engage with. Potentially putting my life at risk, I decided to push Kev on the why. 'Why is it, Kev, that you believe in this product? Why was it that you bought this business?'

The product features kept on coming, but I persisted. Finally, frustrated and red in the cheeks, big, burly Kev leaned across the table towards me with a clenched fist and hard eyes and said (expletives removed): 'I've seen too many of my mates go bust over the years because they weren't using a system like this. They didn't manage their business. They didn't have a system to manage their projects and financials. Many of them lost their homes, their marriages broke down, one of my mates topped himself. That's why I bought this business. Builders need to use this system to help them manage their business so they don't go bust.'

Yes! Finally we had a *why*. Kev and his business can genuinely say: 'This is our industry and we are committed to it. We care about builders growing and successfully managing their business. We want to significantly reduce the number of builders that go bust. To stay afloat, you need the right tool and advice. And by the way, our software is that tool, and we can provide the advice.'

––––––

The Endeavour Foundation in Australia[47] is a large non-profit organisation with tens of thousands of customers with intellectual disabilities. They provide in-home services and care and supported accommodation, as well as education and employment opportunities. In mid-2018 they changed how they described what they do – the services and functional products they provide. Their purpose now was to help their customers 'Live their best lives', to help their customers 'dream' and achieve what was 'possible' for them. They now had a level 1 value proposition that resonated with of their two core customer groups: (1) customers with intellectual disabilities, and (2) family, carers, and supporters of the first customer group. The *why* was to have these people 'Imagine what's possible'... and by the way, we provide services that can help you achieve what's possible for you.

In an earlier chapter I mentioned the start-up superannuation fund Spaceship. In attracting the 11,000 presubscribed customers to their fund pre-launch, they did not talk about expected fund performance, or investment returns, or fee structures. Instead, they connected with a segment of the population that were rejecting the old, established approach to fund management. Rather than investing in the big banks and mining companies, they chose investment strategies that this disaffected generation could connect with: Facebook, Amazon. Much of the rhetoric Spaceship used was emotional, claiming that the previous generation had left the younger generation in a poor financial and economic position. Thousands of customers joined Spaceship because they connected with this message. Not because the fund would perform better, but because it *felt* right.

To develop a level 1 value proposition, you need to answer one main question for your chosen customer group: *Why should they engage with you?* It won't be about your product or service, unless a friend, colleague, or family member has suggested it to them. It will be about a reason to connect on values, or principles, or a cause.

Level 1 value proposition template

The following template will help you to clearly articulate this *why*.

Try describing your story – Why are you doing this? Provide a narrative about why your business exists and for whom.
What genuine position can you take in the marketplace that will resonate with your chosen customer group? What messages will increase the depth of engagement with these customers?
How are you changing the world and making it better for your customers?
Now summarise these stories into a succinct statement. Why should someone identify or connect emotionally with you and your business?

Level 2 value proposition development

With our level 1 value proposition in place we can start to answer the next question the customer would ask: 'Okay, but why should I buy your product or service?' The level 2 value proposition is where most of us are more comfortable, as it tends to be more tangible. First, it will probably describe the features of your product or service.

The next question the customer might have is: 'Well, why should I buy your product or service as opposed to the alternatives available to me?' Here we will be describing points of difference against other choices the customer might have. Also, here we could add in how your existing customers describe the reasons they continue to use your products or services. Your Customer Value Maps are a great source of ideas for the level 2 value proposition.

Level 2 value propositions need to be very specific for each customer group and each product or service line. They also need to be aligned with what your customers value, so be specific about the results or goals they can achieve. Describe the typical results with statistics, facts, and case studies.

Provide a promise about the experience they will have as your customer, and, if appropriate, describe the community they could belong to. Many large business-to-business software firms have recognised the value of community and established large User Group get-togethers. Pre-customers ('prospects') are invited to the User Groups so that they can feel part of the community before they become a customer. These community activities provide a lot of social proof for those considering purchasing the software, as well as letting them know they won't be on their own if they do.

Features, advantages, and benefits

Many level 2 value propositions are derived from considering features, advantages, and benefits[48]. Here is a table of the basic definitions.

- *Features* – The facts, data, product characteristics, and even quality statistics on the product
- *Advantages* – How products, services, or their features can be used or can help the customer
- *Benefits* – How products or services meet the explicit needs expressed by the customer

Here are some examples:

Feature	Advantages	Benefit
The timber uses a non-toxic treatment.	Safe to use in a wide range of applications.	Can be used in: · Children's play areas · Playground equipment · Council-specified applications Can be disposed of in landfill.
Our software for builders interfaces with supplier pricing.	No need to manually update material costs from suppliers.	The margin on your job will not be eroded through increased costs from suppliers.
The coaching service will be provided by an expert.	The expert has performed the same role as you before.	You will be able to avoid common traps and mistakes in your role.

Level 2 value propositions on their own may have little impact, especially if competitors are saying the same things. If you cannot articulate the specific difference between your offering and another, then you are in trouble. However, if your Level 1 VP is truly engaging, then customers will really only be looking for justification for making the decision.

In business-to-business contexts, selling organisations are finding that they need to go well beyond benefits. As mentioned earlier, research by CEB (www.cebglobal.com) has found that companies seeking to engage with business buyers need to provide genuine insights.[49] In an information-drenched world, selling organisations need to be able to communicate unique insights specifically relevant to the customer as part of their value proposition.

There is a great example on YouTube of how a discussion of features, advantages, and benefit can flow in quite natural communication. American blues guitarist Kenny Wayne Shepherd introduces the Fender American Professional Stratocaster (for Fender Guitars).[50] About five minutes into the video he introduces the new narrow-tall frets (feature). He then describes the advantage of these frets: they give the player more space when playing chords, especially high up on the neck. They are also tall enough to give you plenty of separation between your fingers and the fretboard so that you are not slowed down by friction. Then he says, 'That's really important to me because...' (here comes the benefit) 'that enables you to play faster and to bend larger.' The following table outlines all the features, advantages, and benefits covered in the video.

Feature	Advantages	Benefits
New narrow-tall frets	• More space between the frets, especially high on the neck • Separation between your fingers and the fretboard	• More room to work with • Does not slow you down • Play faster • Bend larger
Pop-in tremolo arm	• Just pops in • No need to screw it in • Eliminates noise associated with other tremolo systems	• Saves time: 'Really fast in the middle of a show' • Virtually silent, no noise
Treble bleed circuit	• Instrument tone does not change as the volume increases or decreases • Keeps the high-end frequency	• Have the same sound in the full range of volume • 'You keep that high end, which is really important for me'

Level 2 value propositions are developed for products and services for specific customer groups. If you've established your features/advantages/benefits approach, it can then be reversed to produce a Level 2 value proposition:

If you are a guitarist that wants to play faster and bend larger, you will need more space between your fingers on the fretboard. You can get this on the American Professional Stratocaster because it has the new feature of narrow-tall frets.

Importantly, a statement such as the one above qualifies the customer first. If you are not a customer that wants those benefits, then you do not need to know about the advantages of the feature. And this is the mistake most organisations make with value propositions – they lead with their features. So often these are not meaningful for the customer. As Peter Drucker once said, 'The customer rarely buys what the company thinks it is selling.'[51]

Developing level 2 value propositions

So how do we go about developing our own level 2 value propositions? How are they different from level 1? This is all about getting into the detail of your offerings, the benefits your customers will receive. Identify the combinations of benefits that your customers will realise, recognising the jobs they are trying to get done and the results or goals they want achieve. Describe the experiences you want them to have and consider any community benefits they will acquire.

It is here that we need to address customers' questions about why they should buy your products and services, both in an absolute sense, and in comparison to any alternatives they have before them. It is here that we must provide the rational answers to the customer's questions.

Level 2 value proposition template

Use this process and template as a guide:

1. Choose a customer group that you want to engage with from your Customer Strategy.

2. Develop the Customer Value Map for this customer group.

3. Fill in the first two columns of the template below: list the features, advantages, , aligned to the experience, results/goals achieved, and outcomes.

4. Now go back to the top of your list and for each one, consider: Is this a point of difference to the alternatives available to the customer?

5. Select the features/advantages/functions that are best aligned with customer outcomes, and where you have a point of difference in the customer's marketplace.

6. Use the selected features/advantages/functions to produce a level 2 value proposition.

Features, Advantages	Experience, Results/Goals Achieved, Outcomes (Benefits)	A Point of Difference? (Yes/No/Maybe)	Select (Y/N)

Now, select one of the rows with a point of difference. In the box below, write your level 2 value proposition (along the lines of the example on the previous page). First identify the customer and the benefits they will get from the advantages you (your product or service) provide, then describe the product/service and the features that enable those benefits. You may also add in here any technical specifics that demonstrate the benefit.

Level 2 Value Proposition

Remember, level 2 value proposition statements on their own provide little benefit. Don't make the mistake of thinking this is what will convince the customer to buy from you. But when a customer has already engaged with your level 1 value proposition, they will then be looking for level 2 statements to help them justify their decision.

Summary

Authentic value propositions are customer centric. It starts with identifying your awesome customers as part of your Customer Strategy. It's about appealing not to lots of customers, but to the few that get the value you are offering.

We saw that there are two levels of value propositions. Level 1 is about emotionally connecting with your customer group and the genuine reason why. Level 2 then provides details that allows the customer to engage more deeply with the service or product you are offering.

When it comes to implementing your value propositions, context is everything. By approaching the development of your value propositions in the manner described in this chapter, you will be better prepared to apply your value propositions to the various contexts needed – which will then align your Customer Strategy to the delivery of value for your customers.

———

Templates available for this chapter:

1. Level One Value Proposition Template
2. Level Two Value Proposition Template

CHAPTER EIGHT
THE DELIVERY OF VALUE

The third phase of our business model is all about *delivery of value*. It is the action or 'doing' part of the framework. Remember, this 'doing' is about how we deliver value for customers and needs to be informed by our chosen Customer Strategy and our specific value propositions. Delivery of value to customers means delivering what we have promised to deliver (in our value propositions) to each of our chosen customer groups. One of the keys to the delivery of value is congruence. Action at the front line must be aligned with the overarching business intent and strategy. All the business' resources must be focused on realising the Customer Strategy. What the customer experiences as delivered value must match with what was promised.

Moving into Phase 3

Within the context of the delivery of value, we have specific, deep topics and functions that need to be informed by and aligned with the Customer Strategy. These include:

- Customer service and experience management
- Process management
- Performance measurement and improvement

- Coordinated communications (marketing and sales)

- Sales (engagement) tactics to support the Customer Strategy

- Customer service design and excellence

- Customer retention.

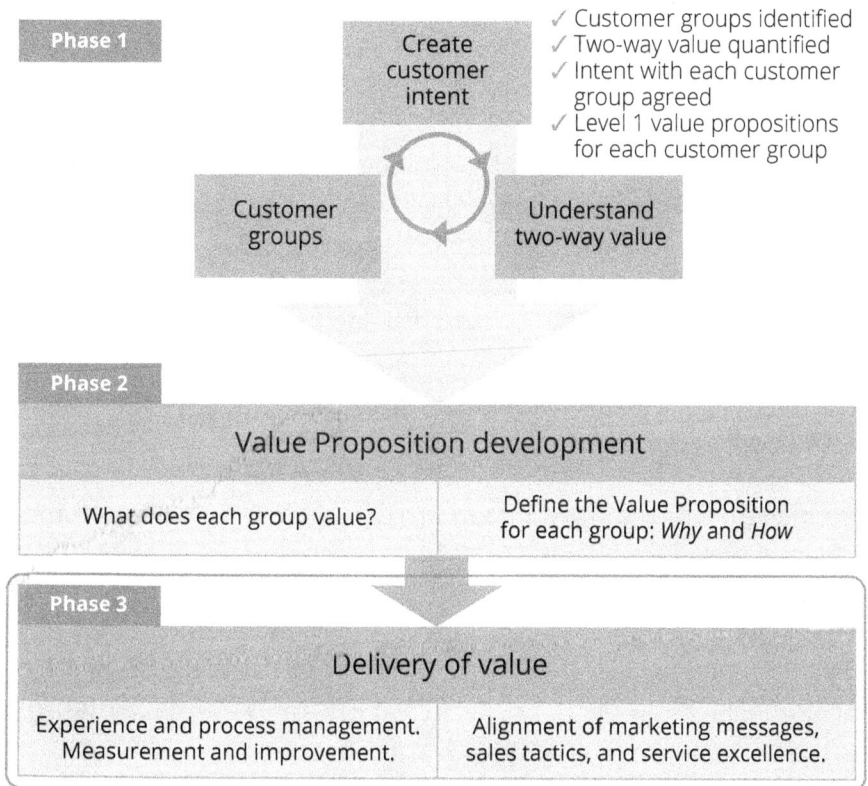

A book could be written on each of these topics! However, our focus here is on *profit by design*: how businesses can unlock the value of their customer portfolio and create a customer portfolio full of profitable promoters. Therefore, we will pay more attention to how we bring customers into our portfolio, and we will use the 'Architecture for Customer Engagement' to understand all the parts of the system that need to be synchronised.

But first, let's recognise a few important points about the delivery of value.

Customer experience is critical for all organisations. As we have already discussed, we are in the experience economy – an economy driven by customers' perceived experiences. For better or worse, customers' perceptions of experience drive their decision making. Experience management is not a standalone exercise for any organisation; it must be informed by the Customer Strategy. If not – that is if customer experiences are designed for *all* customers – service and experience delivery will often cost more than they return.

Alignment is key in the design of all customer communications, service, and processes. The process flow and all communications need to come together for the customer as a seamless experience. Too often business processes are aligned around structures or functions. The focus for alignment should always be the customer and their journey. This is critical if you are to be congruent with your promised value. In terms of communication, Matthews and Schneck put it this way: 'Value messaging is the glue that aligns enablement services. People need value messages all along the customer's path.'[52] Messaging means not only direct communications, but all the ways in which you interact with the customer – every aspect of the how and the what.

Measurement is key to understanding what to improve, and where improvement efforts are having an impact. The goal here is to establish a measurement framework for understanding how well you are performing across the customer journeys and why, and then develop insights on how to improve in specific chosen areas. Dean Spitzer is acknowledged as one of the world's leading authorities on measuring and managing performance. In his seminal work, *Transforming Performance Measurement*, he says, 'The measurement system triggers virtually everything that happens in an organization, both strategic and tactical. This is because all the other organizational systems are ultimately based on what the measurement system is telling the other systems to do.'[53] The performance measurement methodology I use is PuMP® (Performance Measurement Process), developed by Australian statistician and measurement specialist Stacey Barr.[54] This method uses a comprehensive set of tools and techniques to develop a robust framework of causal results and measures that provide feedback on how your business systems are performing.

Customer retention is a goal rather than a function. Retention is the result or outcome of doing all the other things well – aligning all the components of your value delivery system (such as acquisition, service, and communication) to achieve the goals in your Customer Strategy and grow a profitable customer portfolio. Retaining more of your awesome customers is a key driver of long-term profitability. And to retain awesome customers, you must deliver value for them.

Let's now turn to 'sales tactics', also known as 'customer acquisition', or, as I prefer to call it, customer engagement.

The Architecture for Customer Engagement

So many businesses put a huge amount of effort into the development of their products and services. Yet, when the product is ready, it's a quick handball to the sales and marketing teams and an instruction to 'Go sell it!' This worked just fine during the last, product-centric centuries. The focus was on mass production at lowest cost, and from there it was simply a matter of distributing the product to eagerly awaiting consumers, who would be converted by armies of salespeople. Revenue was the goal, and profit the consequence. Not anymore!

Using a framework to deliver on our Customer Strategy and design our engagement with customers will help us ensure the goal of a profitable customer portfolio is realised *on purpose*. This is not about closing deals, but opening relationships with your awesome customers, with whom there is optimal two-way value exchange. The result? Profitable customers who are promoters of what you do.

Let's start with a quick overview of the Architecture for Customer Engagement on the next page, then we will dive into the details of how to apply and build it.

ARCHITECTURE
FOR CUSTOMER ENGAGEMENT

The conversation that attracts and keeps your awesome customer

Do the results suggest changes to the initial inputs?

Progressive improvement

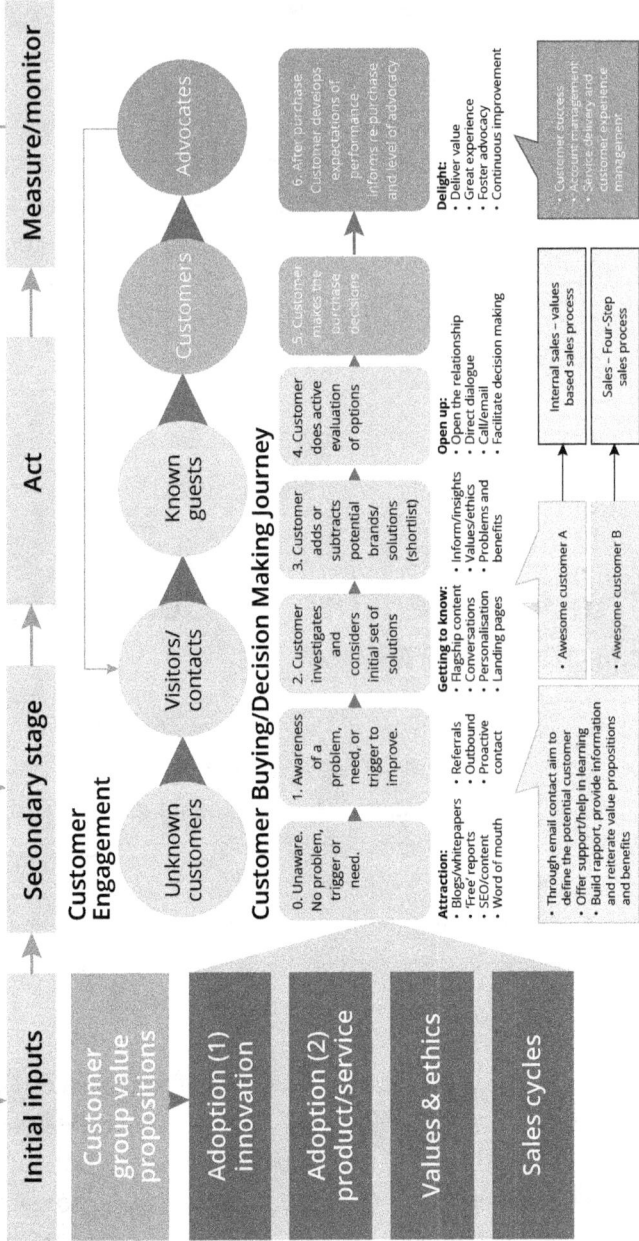

Initial inputs	→	Secondary stage	→	Act	→	Measure/monitor

Customer Engagement

Unknown customers → Visitors/ contacts → Known guests → Customers → Advocates

Customer group value propositions

Adoption (1) innovation

Adoption (2) product/service

Values & ethics

Sales cycles

Customer Buying/Decision Making Journey

0. Unaware. No problem, trigger or need.

1. Awareness of a problem, need, or trigger to improve.

2. Customer investigates and considers initial set of solutions

3. Customer adds or subtracts potential brands/ solutions (shortlist)

4. Customer does active evaluation of options

5. Customer makes the purchase decisions

6. After purchase Customer develops expectations of performance informs re-purchase and level of advocacy

Attraction:
- Blogs/whitepapers
- 'Free' reports
- SEO/content
- Word of mouth
- Referrals
- Outbound
- Proactive contact

Getting to know:
- Flagship content
- Conversations
- Personalisation
- Landing pages
- Inform/insights
- Values/ethics
- Problems and benefits

Open up:
- Open the relationship
- Direct dialogue
- Call/email
- Facilitate decision making

Delight:
- Deliver value
- Great experience
- Foster advocacy
- Continuous improvement

- Customer success
- Account management
- Service delivery and customer experience management

- Through email contact aim to define the potential customer
- Offer support/help in learning
- Build rapport, provide information and reiterate value propositions and benefits

- Awesome customer A
- Awesome customer B

Internal sales – values based sales process

Sales – Four-Step sales process

Let's start on the left with the *Initial Inputs*. The initial input stage begins with identifying the awesome customer groups in your Customer Strategy and then getting your *Customer Group Value Propositions* right for those customers at two levels (why you and then what you do). Continuing down the left column, we come to *Adoption (1): Innovation*. This is about knowing what customer market you are appealing to – early adopters? The majority? Knowing what stage of customer adoption your products or services are in will be a big factor in how you find your awesome customers.

Next, you need to consider *Adoption (2): Product/Service* – how you want your customers to adopt your products/services. This has to match with your strategy for initially engaging your customers, and with the *Values and Ethics* you want to be known for. Engagement with your customers has to feel right. Remember, people buy emotionally, *then* seek rational information to support that decision. Finally, you'll need to consider where in the *Sales Cycle* your product/service is sitting.

Once the initial inputs are figured out, you then need to understand how your awesome customers make decisions. To the right of the *Initial Inputs* is the *Secondary Stage*, which focuses on aligning the optimal engagement activity to support the goal of creating profitable promoters. We'll look at this in detail in the next chapter. Congruence across the engagement activity is critical. If, at any stage during the engagement process, the customer gets the *feeling* something isn't right – that there is incongruence – they will opt out of engaging with you.

Architecture for Customer Engagement – initial inputs

Adoption (1): innovation

Let's first consider the types of customers you will be dealing with from the perspective of how innovative your product or service is in the marketplace. In 1962, Everett Rogers published the 'Diffusion of innovations' theory, which separates customers into one of five groups on the basis of how readily they adopt a new product or service.[55] This widely accepted theory has many applications. It has stood the test of time because it gets to the heart of human behaviour.

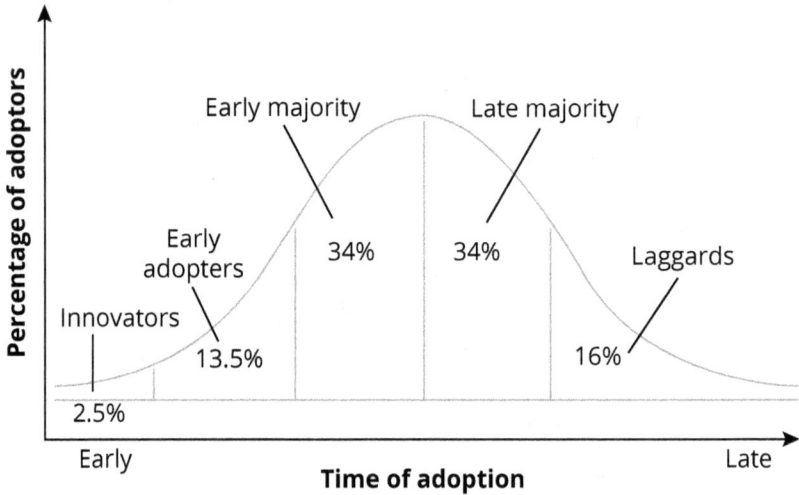

There are various customer types, with different adoption attitudes based on their preferences. Let's start by understanding what each of the stages of product uptake looks like, before going into how to tailor your strategy for each stage.

Innovators represent around 2.5% of the available market for new products and services. These are the people who are almost obsessed with trying out new ideas and products. They want new products and experiences *because* they are new. A big part of the value they get consists in being first.

Early Adopters represent about 13.5% of the population. These are distinct from Innovators because they are much more reliant on group norms and values. Typically they are also more orientated to the local community and are likely to be opinion leaders. They are, however, influenced by Innovators. They watch Innovators to determine when to adopt something new.

The next 34% are the *Early Majority*, and they are very deliberate about how they buy. They are likely to collect more information and evaluate more brands than the earlier groups. The buying habits of the majority are very different to customers in the early stages of adoption. The Early Majority will not purchase any new innovation without first seeing it being picked up and endorsed by the Early Adopters. This behaviour is so marked that author Geoffrey Moore refers to the 'line' between the early adopters and the early majority as a 'chasm' – a chasm that so many hopeful businesses and products have fallen into, never to be heard of again[56]. To get the attention of the majority, organisations need to use the stories, testimonials, and social proof of the earlier groups.

A few years ago, Microsoft released Windows 10 for free. It was, of course, the Innovators who downloaded the new operating system first. Microsoft got feedback on how it worked and made the few tweaks needed to keep the Innovators happy... then the Early Adopters got in on the free download. But why? Why would Microsoft offer their new flagship product for free? Well, by moving quickly through the Innovator cohort and into the Early Adopters, Microsoft could then offer the product for sale to the Early Majority, and this majority customer market is (for Microsoft) where the money is. By offering the Windows 10 product for free, they got to the majority earlier and crossed 'the chasm'.

The *Late Majority* accounts for the next 34%. They adopt a new product mainly because a lot of their friends have already adopted the product. This group is reliant on norms, and adoption is essentially the result of pressure to conform. Let's not be dismissive of these customers just because they adopt new things after everyone else. These people, along with the Early Majority, are just that – the majority. Most of us, and our customers, fall into one of these categories. So once our products and services have matured, these customers will make up a fair chunk of our profitable promoters.

The ultimate resistance comes from *Laggards* – the final 16%. Ironically, they share a similarity with innovators – a disregard for group norms! Their purchasing decisions are made in terms of the past. By the time Laggards adopt 'new' products, they have probably been superseded. By the time Laggards adopt, it is probably because they have no choice. We are starting to hear from Laggards in regions of Australia where copper telephone landline services are being phased out as they are forced to (finally!) join the mobile revolution.

The key message from the 'diffusion of innovations' theory for the design of customer engagement is that customers in the early stages of adoption simply *buy*. Customers in the later stages need a nudge to buy, and in many cases this nudge might be the type of engagement that intrudes into the space of the customer and then draws their attention towards your offerings.[57] The optimal type of intrusion is advocacy from friends, colleagues, and family members.

———

So how do we approach each type of customer? If your product or service is in the early stage of adoption, which means it will appeal to Innovators and then Early Adopters, the challenge for customer engagement lies in finding the customer. If your offering is truly innovative, then it will only appeal to 2.5% (approximately) of your available market! A traditional marketing approach aimed at all your potential customers will be wasted. The essential engagement activity here is to identify the Innovators in your market. From there, the engagement approach will entail approaching potential (Innovator) customers with a quiet word about how exciting and new this offering is. Remember, the challenge of getting Innovators to buy is in finding the right customer and presenting the new thing. If you've found the right customer, they *will* buy.

Similarly, for Early Adopters the aim will be to identify and locate these customers. From there, engagement will be relatively easy to obtain, as long as the message appeals to the Early Adopter. And that message is something like: 'We can show you how Innovators have used our new offering. Be one of the first in your market to have/use this new product or service.' We use the stories and lessons learned from the Innovators to empower Early Adopters to buy.

When we approach the Early Majority, we again use stories from Early Adopters who have used the product or service, but for majority-type customers the most important aspect of these stories is that they provide social proof.

In order to design the optimal customer engagement activity – from a diffusion of innovation perspective – you must know what market your offering is in. If it is truly in the early stages of adoption, focus on learning how to find the right customers and share the innovative products and services with them. If your offerings are in the later stages of adoption, ensure you develop the skills and capabilities to match the needs and attitudes of these customers.

Adoption (2): product/service

This input into the design of customer engagement is about *how* the customer adopts and uses your product or service. Customers (businesses or consumers) that adopt a new product or service will typically pass along the following path.

1. *Awareness*. The consumer or business becomes aware of a new product that can meet a need or a replace a product they are currently using.

2. *Knowledge*. The customer then seeks knowledge about the new product or service, for example by searching the web or talking with friends, family, or colleagues.

3. *Evaluation*. Now the customer will evaluate the options available. Do the features, advantages, and benefits of the new product or service match their (perceived) needs? Do the (perceived) values of the business align with those of the customer?

4. *Decision*. The customer makes the decision to buy the product or service, and tries it out.

5. *Adoption*. If everything is acceptable to the customer, considered in light of perceived alternatives, then they adopt the new product or service.

How we interact with the potential customer during this engagement process will significantly affect their likelihood of adopting the service or product.

———

Let's look at two examples.

A business becomes aware of a new software package that may overcome some of the frustrations they are experiencing with their current system. Through a Google search they find a local seller and make some enquiries. A salesperson makes contact on behalf of the seller and agrees to see the customer to provide a demonstration. If this salesperson has a sales leader with good values and ethics, they will follow suit and present themselves and the business honestly, describing what the new system can actually do. But what if this person's salary has a high proportion of commission and they are not involved in installing the software? If the salesperson makes assertions about the product that are not completely true, and the customer buys based on these statements, then when the delivery team turns up to install the software and train the customer's team there will be problems. The software manufacturer may have to reconfigure the software to make it do what the salesperson said, or reduce the price, or provide some other sort of remedy. Or maybe the customer just has to use the system the way it is delivered, and live with their expectations unmet. Either way, the salesperson's actions have cost the selling business – reputational damage, implementation costs, and potential loss of future revenue based on the potential for negative word of mouth.

Credit card providers want customers to use their card more often than any other card. In fact, the goal is that customers use *only* this card. If a salesperson for a credit card provider 'oversells' the benefits of their card (exaggerating about where it can be used, for example) and does not fully inform the customer of all the charges and fees and how to avoid them, then once the customer starts to use the card they will (most likely) be unhappy with their choice, tell lots of people about how they were misinformed, and not use the credit card in the way the provider wants them to. The salesperson's role is to ensure the customer is fully informed and empowered to use the credit card in the way the provider wants them to – and this means telling the customer about fees and other unpleasant things. The objective is to have the customer take the card and use it. If the card is sold but not used, it does not achieve the company's goals (and may even work against them).

Our goal is to engage with potential customers that will grow the portion of profitable promoters in our customer portfolio. Every part of the customer engagement process has to be in harmony with ensuring our new customer will not only adopt and use our products and services, but also become an advocate of what we do.

Values and ethics

Any discussion on optimal customer engagement activity must include consideration of values and ethics.[58] There must be universal congruence in the way the organisation presents itself to customers – congruence between the activity and the brand. The customer will attribute a set of values and ethics to a brand based on how the organisation behaves. Behaviours are observable and very real for customers.

Behaviours reflect values

We display our values in the language we use and the actions we take. Behaviours are evidence of the values, beliefs, and assumptions below the surface. Sure, some people try to disguise their true beliefs, but the underlying assumption there is that they can actually fool people. When a business says that it 'values people', we can assess the truth in that by looking at how they treat people. This might mean different things for different customers. Some may look for evidence that they treat their employees well (whatever that subjectively means to them). Others may want the organisation to treat its customers well (however they define that). Still others may interpret 'values people' to mean that the organisation must source its products and supplies from businesses with good practices – fair wages and conditions, and no child labour.

When deciding on an ethical code of practice, a good way to start is to list the values you want to be known for, then describe the behaviours that reflect that value. For example:

Value	Behaviours that reflect this value
We trust our people.	• We treat people fairly in all interactions. • We provide above-average benefits for our people.
We value our customers.	• We always communicate honestly. • We aim to deliver value for our customers each and every time. • We always act in our customers' best interests.
We believe in conscious capitalism.	• We only source supplies from organisations that meet the international standards for labour. • We give back to our communities. • We respect and love our environment, and preserve and protect it.

Organisations get into public relations strife when their behaviour does not reflect the values they espouse. Businesses lose a portion of their customers when their behaviour does not reflect their (perceived) values. Not only will existing customers leave, but importantly, customers in the initial engagement phase will opt out, as it just doesn't feel right. Customers make decisions emotionally.

Alignment of values with sales and service people

Though it is widely accepted that the behaviours a sales or service person should align with the values and ethics of the business, it is often not discussed within organisations. When the customer purchases, there needs to be congruence between the behaviour of the salespeople and the expected ongoing relationship between the customer and the brand. And it doesn't end when the customer leaves the store! If the sales experience is incongruent with the post-sales experience, this causes buyer dissonance, which reduces longer-term value for the business.

If you go into a Vodafone store, you should instantly get a sense of energy from the salespeople. Vodafone sales teams talk about RED, the vibrancy and energy of their brand (which rests in part on past symbolism of the colour red – for example, its association with Formula 1 racing and sports clubs such as Manchester United). The salespeople in the Vodafone store are keen to represent their brand in this way because they know that the customers coming into their store have already been in some way attracted by that branding. The situation is very different, of course, when you enter a high-end store like Tiffany's. Here, you are likely to be formally greeted by a sales assistant with immaculate personal appearance, not an energetic person in a bright red polo asking 'How ya doin'?' Each company has tailored its sales approach to match its branding and its customer expectations.

Sales and service leaders need to design desired behaviours for the team with the value attributes of the brand in mind and ensure these are understood and practised across every part of the organisation. This will provide alignment throughout the customer experience, which will in turn provide more profitable promoters within the customer portfolio and better results for the business.

Ethics in practice

Unfortunately, ethics are often only discussed after a problem arises. By then it's already too late. Ethical discussions need to occur during the design of the customer engagement practice. Potential ethical dilemmas need to be identified as risks, and mitigated. It is about taking a conscious approach to the interactions you want to have with customers, rather than just letting things happen.

Let's take the example of Wells Fargo, the second-largest bank in the USA. Wells Fargo was fined 185 million USD by the financial services Consumer Protection Bureau early in September 2016 after employees were accused of opening around 2 million accounts/credit cards without customers' knowledge.[59] Wells Fargo employees had been opening and funding 'fraudulent accounts' so that they could meet their sales and cross-selling targets, allegedly for 4–5 years. It all began to unravel when customers picked up on extra account fees. Since then the bank has 'terminated' more than 5,000 employees, many executives have 'retired', and the CEO has resigned. While Wells Fargo will undoubtedly end up paying hundreds of millions of dollars in fines and legal fees, their biggest cost has to be the loss of trust, and not only with their existing customers. Any potential customer would have to think long and hard before opening a relationship with Wells Fargo.

Similarly, the 2018 Financial Services Royal Commission in Australia found mountains of evidence of poor practice by financial services companies.[60] Reports claim that 'poor culture and misaligned incentives were the key cause of misconduct.' Organisations sold insurance policies that customers could never claim on, took advantage of risk-averse superannuation customers by paying them much less than market rates, and the list goes on. In an ABC News article, ANZ Bank Chief Executive said many employees 'dehumanise' work, as 'they don't see a customer'.[61] He said, 'There have been ethical lapses … 50,000 people come to work every day at ANZ. Less than 20 percent of them ever see a customer …' If the employees at ANZ don't see a customer, what do they see? Products, budgets, KPIs, plans, and projects.

Don't think for a moment that these are isolated examples. CustomerThink, 'the world's largest online community dedicated to customer-centric strategy' releases an annual Sales Ethics Hall of Shame.[62] The list is huge and many of the brands are quite familiar.

The time to discuss values and ethics is when we are developing our Architecture for Customer Engagement. Not when things go wrong, or customers are affected, or the issues become public.

Sales cycle

The sales cycle encompasses the length of time from the beginning of the sales process to the decision being made. Therefore, the sales cycle can be anything from a few minutes to a few years! If you are selling car insurance policies over the phone, you have about five minutes to help the customer make a decision that is in line with the company you represent. But if you're selling passenger jets, the sales cycle could well be years. The sales cycle has always been important for selling organisations, but was particularly so when the sales cycle used to align with the investigative stage of purchasing.

Not that long ago, salespeople would start the process of buying with a customer. Not so today. Research (and common sense) is showing that in most purchasing decisions, the customer does not involve a sales representative until about two-thirds of the way through their buying journey (if they do at all). This is critically important for how we design our engagement with our chosen customers. In today's experience economy, the sales cycle might more usefully be understood as the length of time the customer is actively engaged with your representatives.

We need to understand how our customers buy – the process they go through – and design our activity around that. If you get to talk with a customer prior to them making a decision, then consider:

- How long will that conversation take – do you have minutes, or hours of detailed briefings?
- Is it one conversation or many over time?
- What assumptions and information may the customer already have prior to the conversation?

As a general rule, the shorter the sales cycle, the tighter the engagement processes, scripts, and prompts need to be. There is no time to 'wing it'; the customer engagement needs to be very focused. With longer sales cycles, we can consider using higher-level process flows and broader methods of interactions.

Summary

In this chapter we have covered the key principles in the delivery of value. Once we have figured out our Customer Strategy, we need to bring it to life in the delivery of value for the customer, which will in turn achieve a higher value customer portfolio for the organisation.

Before we can design our strategies for customer engagement, we must carefully consider the five initial inputs into the Architecture for Customer Engagement:

1. Customer group value propositions
2. Adoption (1): innovation
3. Adoption (2): product/service
4. Values and ethics
5. Sales cycle

We must ensure that we have considered where our customers might be in the adoption of innovation, and how we would like our customers to adopt our product or services. We must commit to behaviours we know will positively reflect our values and reduce the risk of ethical dilemmas for our employees. And finally, we must take into account the length and nature of the sales cycle when implementing a customer engagement strategy.

Now we are ready to enter the secondary stage, where we will design the optimal activities to build a customer portfolio full of profitable promoters.

––––––

Templates available for this chapter:

1. Adoption (1): Innovation template
2. Adoption (2): Product/service template
3. Values and behaviours template
4. Sales team ethics template

CHAPTER NINE
ENGAGING CUSTOMERS

Our Customer Strategy determined which customers we need to work with to ensure we continue to fill our customer portfolio with profitable promoters. In the previous chapter we looked into the initial stages of the Architecture for Customer Engagement, which guided our thinking on how to design our engagement with customers. In this chapter, we bring the elements of the Architecture for Customer Engagement together.

Before starting this chapter, work through the initial inputs of the Architecture for Customer Engagement for a selected customer group that you want to grow. Develop the value propositions for this group, determine where these customers fall in the adoption curve, and understand the challenge in engaging with them. Consider how you ideally want your customers to use your products/services, how you want to be perceived from a values and ethics perspective, and what the typical sales cycle is.

Now we're ready to look into the overarching approach to engaging with our chosen customers.

Architecture for Customer Engagement – secondary stage

As mentioned above, the initial inputs in the Architecture for Customer Engagement allow us to get the context right prior to the design. Who are the customers; what stage of adoption are they in; how do we want them to use our products and services? This is also our chance to mindfully describe the values and ethics we want to be known for. These initial inputs provide a good foundation for us to look into the process of engaging our chosen customers.

Customer Engagement

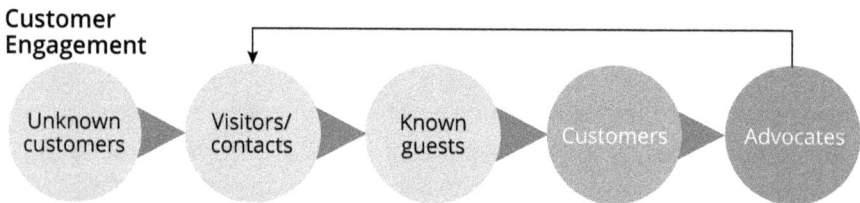

Unknown customers → Visitors/contacts → Known guests → Customers → Advocates

Let's change our philosophical lens and language on this. We do not want to think of our awesome customers as 'prospects', or 'leads', or 'deals' waiting to be 'closed'. These are *people* – people whom we want to add to our customer portfolio, who will get the value we deliver and therefore become profitable for us and promoters of what we do. Let's perceive them initially as *Unknown Customers*, who may be open to a potential two-way value exchange that is mutually beneficial. When they come to us, let's see them as *Visitors* or *Contacts* and see if we can get to know them better. Now we can think of these people as *Known Guests* – people we would (theoretically!) invite into our homes. Through discussions on the mutual exchange of value, they become *Customers* (if you'd rather call these people *Clients*, go right ahead). But this is not the end. If we have done our work well, then they will become *Advocates* – profitable members of our customer portfolio. Our goal is not to close deals, but to open relationships with awesome customers who become profitable promoters.

Now, with these customers identified in the right way, let's look into how they buy – their decision-making and buying journey.

Customer Buying/Decision Making Journey

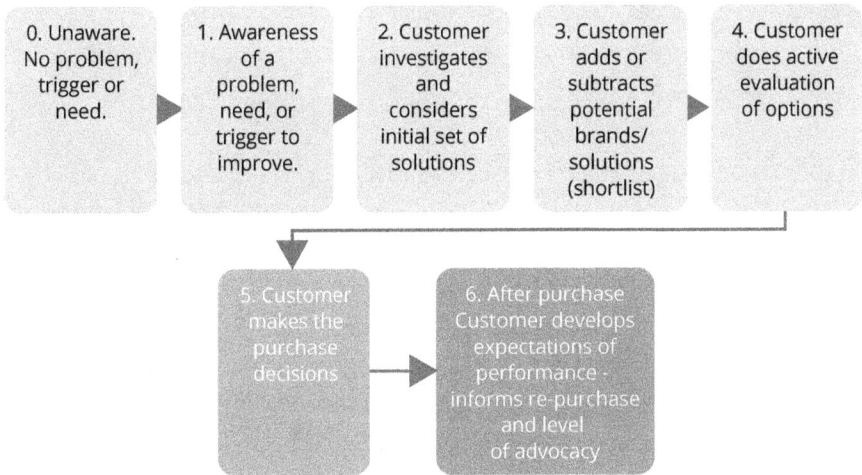

0. Unaware. No problem, trigger or need.	1. Awareness of a problem, need, or trigger to improve.	2. Customer investigates and considers initial set of solutions	3. Customer adds or subtracts potential brands/ solutions (shortlist)	4. Customer does active evaluation of options

5. Customer makes the purchase decisions	6. After purchase Customer develops expectations of performance - informs re-purchase and level of advocacy

We will use the above customer buying journey as typical or representative for a customer group. However, when you come to do this for your specific customer group, remember it may be slightly different depending on the initial inputs.

I have divided this journey into four key stages: *Attract*, *Get to Know*, *Open Up*, and *Delight*. In the health services, certain hospitals that have a good workplace culture and consistently get great patient outcomes become known as 'magnet hospitals' because they *attract* the best practitioners. We want to be known to our potential customers so that, like a magnet, we can attract the right customers. Then, as the customer relationships progresses, we will need to *get to know* one another... and as we do, we will start to *open up* a relationship. If the value exchange seems right, then the customer will choose to take the relationship further. Then it becomes our role to *delight* these customers with a fulfilment of the value we promised. Let's look at each stage in turn.

Attract

In this stage your chosen customer group may be unaware of your offering, because it is new or they don't know you. Your challenge, then, is to find ways of *attracting* them. Not everyone, of course – just those potentially awesome customers. Use language and techniques that will resonate with those customers. If your offering is truly new and innovative, then your challenge is to *find* the Innovators and Early Adopters. Where do they hang out, who/what do they follow? Find them, and inject your new idea into their world.

In the old days of sales and marketing (just a few years back, actually), this stage was called 'Intrude and Engage'. The idea was to literally intrude into the customer's space and get their attention. Ever gone to the movies at the session start time? While you wait for the movie to start, you have to sit through a series of advertisements. Ads based on the 'intrude and engage' idea started in radio and TV years ago and have now invaded our mobile phones, even slowing down our internet browsing. But here's the thing: Intrude and engage very, very rarely works. Even though its proponents may say it's worth it to get a 1-in-10,000 response, it doesn't make sense to me to annoy 9,999 people just to get to one. Intrude and engage is also very costly. John Wanamaker, was a nineteenth century American retailer and marketing pioneer who famously said, 'Half the money I spend on advertising is wasted; the trouble is I don't know which half.'[63] The challenge of attracting customers is in knowing who they are, and what messages will resonate with them.

Jon Hollenberg formed the business Five by Five 12 years ago to provide 'great-looking, high-performing websites for businesses'.[64] When a person is drawn to or referred to Jon he will send you a copy of his book, *Love at First Site*, at no cost (or you can download the audio version on his website). At 130 pages and with lots of illustrations, it's an easy read. And what this book does is show the potential customer Jon and his team's approach to building and managing websites using WordPress. Either the potential customer will buy in to his approach or not. If they do, then they are on the way to becoming an awesome customer for Five by Five, as we already know that their values and approach are a good match. If not, then they are not likely to be the type of customer Five by Five need. At the *Attract* stage, Jon has developed a high-value offering that also helps expedite identification of potentially awesome customers. The customers who progress to the *Get to Know* stage are likely to be aligned with their level 1 value proposition and the way Five by Five design and build websites.

Today, in a very crowded and noisy world full of any and all forms of media and advertising, we need to find ways of *attracting* the customer. It's about pulling them toward you, rather than shoving your product in their faces. This is best done through advocacy within social and working networks. But it can also be done by ensuring that you articulate your level 1 value proposition in a way that resonates with your awesome customers, and that each message adds value in some way. Like a magnet, your awesome customers will be drawn to you. This is why we have to know them, their motivations, and their values – so that our value proposition will ring true for them.

Get to Know

For some customer groups and business contexts, this is where the customer may start to make contact with you, but other customers may still be assessing the value of your offering from a distance. This appraisal will include checking you out online, including any customer reviews, and investigating whether anyone in their networks knows you or your offerings.

The long-term goal is to form a relationship with these customers, but right now you are still getting to know one another. Today I feel it is better to think of this as a 'courtship' than a 'sell job'. Your goal is to ensure you deliver value at each point. You can communicate what you do in many ways, such as through videos, whitepapers, and level 2 value propositions. But always try to include some social proof (ideally, this will also subtly support your level 1 value proposition). What other people and customers are saying about you is important to people trying to get to know you. Potential customers want to know about you as an organisation, not just your products and services. Every bit of information you provide has to reflect value that resonates with your awesome customers.

If your customer *is* making contact with you at this stage, it is critical to be aware that they are not yet ready to make a decision. Hubspot is a USA-based marketing platform that helps companies with marketing and customer relationship management software. If you make contact with Hubspot to find out about their offerings, they will appoint a team member to reach out to you. This person's role is to provide you with information specific to your needs so you can get to know Hubspot. These team members do not sell. They will ask you what you are trying to achieve and in what type of business, and over the following weeks they will provide you with selected content, and potentially introduce to you to other local customers or User Groups. If you get to the point where you want a bit more detailed information, such as a demonstration tailored for you or detailed pricing, only then will your contact hand you over to the 'outside sales team', who will be fully briefed on your journey so far and what you are trying to achieve. For Hubspot, this is where the customer moves out of the *Get to Know* stage and into the *Open Up* stage.

This stage is not about closing a deal. It's about getting to know your customer and opening up a relationship, so behave accordingly. Start the relationship the way you want it to be forever.

Open Up

For most customer buying journeys, this is where dialogue occurs. This is the focus when designing activity for customer engagement. But if your offering is such that your potentially awesome customers can purchase from you without any direct conversations, the same principles still apply. Remember that everything you do must go towards opening a relationship with someone that will be an advocate. There is little value in making a sale to the wrong customer, someone who doesn't get the value you deliver. The gratification of the quick cash hit will soon be lost from lack of advocacy, or even negative word of mouth from this customer – and most of the time the business will never even know.

When we are designing conversations with customers, we need to firstly understand where the customer is coming from. What information, assumptions, ideas, and values do they currently hold? However, we typically cannot ask this straight up, as the customer is probably task focused and not interested in answering what sound like personal questions. They have done their research and they are seeking additional information for the tail end of their decision-making. While we may be looking to build a relationship with them, their focus may not be the same, particularly in shorter sales cycles. In the initial stages of these conversations we are better off to start by seeking to understand the customer's goals. If we know what they want to achieve and what value they are looking for, we can ensure alignment on what we can deliver and when. In this way, we can show respect for their time (and task focus) while also gaining a better understanding of their specific needs and requirements to ensure we can achieve that mutual exchange of value.

This is ostensibly 'the selling process'. But today we need a serious reframe on selling, which has traditionally been seen as something someone 'does' to another. This stage is called *Open Up*, in direct contrast to *close*. To repeat, our goal here is to open relationships with profitable promoters, not close deals. To achieve that goal, we need to ensure our customers are willingly on this journey with us, not being held captive. Having said that, we can still leverage some 'sales' approaches as we design the optimal way to have these conversations (whether face to face or via phone, email, or other messaging).

All 'sales' is human to human. Yet for convenience, we often use the terms B2C and B2B to refer to selling to consumers and business, respectively. It is still human to human! The only difference for B2C is the perception that we are selling to an individual. As customers (as opposed to consumers), while we might be the decision maker, we rarely make these decisions in isolation – friends, family and colleagues are often advisors. In terms of B2B, we are engaging with groups of people making a collective decision. No matter how rational a business-buying team might try to make the process, it is still a collective of emotion-based decisions being made individually. The humanness of it is inescapable. Therefore, across the board, let's call sales *customer engagement*.

Approach to B2C customer engagement

Now, for B2C-style customer engagement, with a relatively short sales cycle on the order of a few minutes, I like to use a process called the 'values-based engagement approach' to help unpack the flow of these conversations. These customers have usually done some research or put you on a shortlist and now they want to clarify some things. Maybe they are even ready to buy something, but often you will still have to help them make that decision.

Just briefly, here are the six steps of the flow of engagement:

1. **Customer contact**. Recognise that the customer comes with knowledge, perceptions, assumptions, expectations, known and unknown needs, and often a particular need in mind.

2. **Rapport**. All relationships start with rapport. Agree on the purpose of the interaction and your willingness to meet the customer's requirements. This step is brief but meaningful. The intent here is to reduce the task focus so the conversation can turn to the next step.

3. **Value assessment**. What does the customer value? What is important to them? What problem can you solve for them? Through open-ended discovery, clarifying questions, and confirming statements, discover what values will drive their decision making. You may also uncover potential future needs.

4. **Risk assessment**. Risk is about costs and effort. How much is the customer willing to pay, and what do they perceive as the optimal value exchange? Do they buy top-end products or services, or go for something less costly? Same with effort – how much effort are they willing to put in to reduce cost? The decision they make will come down to their perception of value.

5. **Solutions and agreement**. Present the solutions, paraphrasing the benefits that align with what the customer values. As far as possible, keep it simple and succinct. Do not list *all* the features and advantages. Make passing references to the level 1 value proposition and link back to level 2 value propositions. Seek agreement that the product/service meets their need. If there is no agreement at this point, loop back to the value assessment to ensure you fully understand what they value.

6. **Sustain the relationship**. If there is agreement, support the decision the customer has made and reassure them that you will deliver what they value. Review and confirm the steps that have been agreed, and set the scene for further interactions. Importantly, check that the customer is happy and satisfied with the experience they have had with you. If agreement cannot be reached, you still need to sustain the relationship. Perhaps you can follow up with

the customer. Think about how you can increase the chance of the customer speaking well of you.

Approach to B2B customer engagement

When it comes to business customers, there are many factors to consider. Our purpose here is not to prescribe B2B sales, but to provide you with a framework and tools to build solid engagement capability. More detailed business sales approaches can be found in *Strategic Selling*, by Miller and Heiman, and *The Challenger Sale*, by Dixon and Adamson (this approach pushes the salesperson to deliver genuine insights of value for the customer).[65] Take a look at these approaches, but remember, this is about aligning your engagement practice with your Customer Strategy. This is not about selling to anyone; rather, it is specifically about building a customer portfolio especially for you that is full of profitable promoters.

Let's briefly consider customers that are part of a buying team in a business. It's useful to recognise the role each person has on the team. Are they decision makers or recommenders? Are they subject-matter experts or do they work in procurement, ensuring the process is compliant? Also important is the context of the purchase. Are they taking an opportunity for improvement, addressing a newly identified problem, or perhaps replacing an existing product or service?

As an overarching approach to engagement with businesses, Neil Rackham identifies four high-level stages businesses go through:[66]

1. **Preliminaries**. The warm-up events before the serious pitch – introductions, early conversation, rapport building between humans. The first few minutes of an interaction leave initial impressions that will influence the rest of the engagement.

2. **Investigation**. This is the most important stage. It is more than collecting data and understanding the customer and their organisation. It is also about understanding their business problems, the results they seek, and the change they desire from the engagement.

3. **Demonstrating capability**. Every engagement will require the selling business to demonstrate the capability to solve the business problems, get the results, and realise the desired change. This is likely to involve presentations, demonstrations, references from other customers, and perhaps even development of a proof of concept.

4. **Obtaining commitment**. Every successful engagement process will end with some sort of commitment from the customer. In larger sales there is likely to be a series of commitments before an order is placed or contracts signed.

These four stages align to the decision-making process for your awesome business customer in your Architecture for Customer Engagement. The key to engaging with businesses is to work through these four stages, completing each stage before moving onto the next.

The purpose of this *Open Up* stage is to ensure we align all of our conversations and activities. We want true congruence across the customer engagement process, from our level 1 value proposition right through to welcoming new customers.

Delight

Once the customer has chosen to become part of your portfolio, your role is to ensure that the mutual two-way value exchange lives on for the customer. Wherever possible, we will seek to delight those customers… but of course, not all customers will be delighted. This seems like an incomplete goal, but remember, this is still part of the outworking of your Customer Strategy. Not every customer is an awesome customer. For some customer groups your goal may be to *Maintain*, recognising an almost transactional relationship. For other groups the intent may be to *Enhance* or *Re-engineer* the relationship. The intent for each group needs to guide how you deliver service, experiences, and value for these customers, with the long-term goal of growing the overall lifetime value and advocacy of the customer portfolio.

Just as customers are not all equal, the service provided for the various customers groups may not be equal. Delivering equally high levels of service and experience to all groups of customers usually means you are overinvesting, and therefore reducing the value of the customer portfolio. In the *Delight* stage of customer engagement, know your Customer Strategy and deliver it. For each customer, you need to be able to identify which customer group they fall into, and deliver the specific intent of the Customer Strategy for that group. Note that all customers, even the *Maintain* group, should get a good experience and the value you promised. This will deliver better retention (and lifetime value) and prevent these customers becoming detractors (which reduces the advocacy value of the portfolio). Customer groups with the intent of *Enhance* or *Re-engineer* also get good service and the promised value, but also the occasional nudge to change the relationship and add value on both ends.

Customer service has long been a focus for organisations, and yet it is often perceived as a cost centre. The Architecture for Customer Engagement approach recognises that the value of service can greatly exceed its costs. Good customer service can differentiate you from alternatives available to your customers. Not only that, but making customer experience the focus of service delivery means you can reach the *hearts* of your customers – the decision-making centre for staying, repurchasing, and providing positive word of mouth. Remember, though, that you only want to retain and grow certain portions of your customer portfolio. So be specific and deliberate with your efforts and investments in service.

For the customer group with the intent of *Grow*, you will need to not only identify them but also predict where they are heading. Often, a customer's behaviour will be a predictor of their intentions. For customers within your *Grow* group, you will need to be able to identify customers at risk of leaving and implement proactive interventions. When a customer contacts you to tell you they are leaving, it's too late. Get smart at predicting your customers' behaviour and proactively reaching out to save the relationship – these *Grow* customer groups are worth it. How you do this will vary from one context to another. Consider your favourite coffee shop. Do they stamp a loyalty card each time you get your caffeine fix? These types of loyalty cards create transactional relationships – 'When I get to the right count of clicks on my card, you owe me a coffee.' Consider an alternative – the savvy coffee shop owner that recognises the regulars and once every couple of weeks surprises them with a coffee on the house.

For organisations that are in the business of providing products and services to other businesses, the *Delight* stage might cover service delivery and account management. For want of a better term, account management is really ongoing engagement with the business customer informed by the Customer Strategy (see the case study in the following section for more on this approach). The effort and resources you put into any contact with customers has to be on purpose. Alignment of all resources will maximise the realisation of results.

Identify those customers that may be willing to provide positive word of mouth. Now, how can you foster that advocacy? How can you help them tell their friends, family, and colleagues about you? Investments in this area will improve the value of the customer portfolio, reduce acquisition costs, and increase retention. We need to be thoughtful about how we do this, and mindful of potential unintended consequences. For example, imagine a local gym offering membership to new customers for a lower weekly cost than existing members. How do you think this makes the loyal existing members feel?

Now imagine the gym offers to give its loyal members two weeks free if they get one of their friends to join. In this case, the member encourages a friend to get fit and also gets some dollars back. But what if the gym offered the two free weeks to the friend instead? Same opportunity cost for the gym, but now both parties get added perceived value – the member gets value from the opportunity to offer the deal to their friend, *and* the friend gets two weeks free. The value exchange has to be perceived as fair to all.

The *Delight* stage is not just about service and ongoing communications. It is about the genuine delivery of your Customer Strategy – the delivery of specific goals, results, and experiences to specific customer groups. The service department is not a cost centre, but a mechanism or system to finetune and increase the value of your customer portfolio.

Implementation: Act, Measure, Monitor

Once we have designed the Architecture for Customer Engagement, we need to implement it. Implementation is often seen as an action that can simply be completed and ticked off. Not so. The Architecture for Customer Engagement is not a once-off, set-and-forget approach, it is ongoing. Development of the initial inputs and execution of the secondary stage are only the first pass of implementation. Once these elements are in place, we then need to ensure that we continually test and finetune our Architecture, including our initial assumptions. Essentially, this process is an action learning cycle where we measure and learn from what is working and what needs improvement.

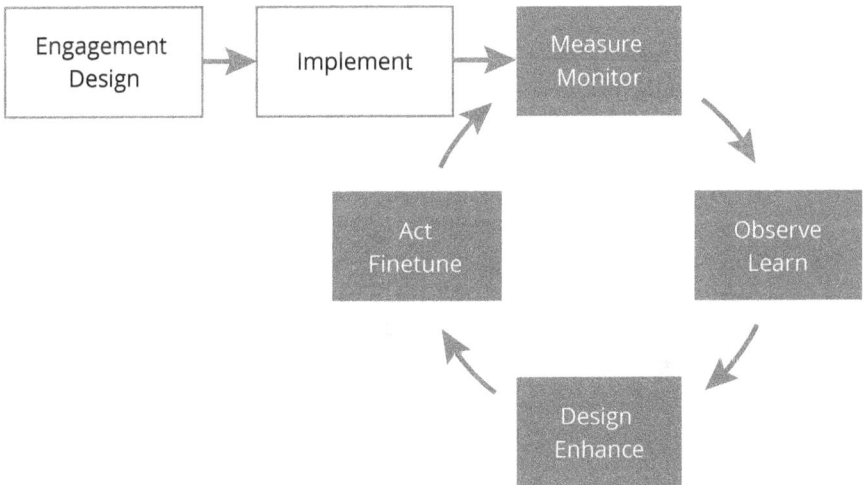

Act

Implementation is not about perfecting the Customer Strategy or the Architecture for Customer Engagement. It is about following a practical model to get moving! Only after you have implemented your Architecture can you start learning about what works and what doesn't. In my experience, implementation can take up to three months. That doesn't mean three months to communicate the Customer Strategy and Architecture for Customer Engagement to everyone. (Hopefully you have engaged your people in the design, so it won't come as a complete surprise!) It means three months to continuously communicate with and support your employees in the implementation.

As humans, our behaviours and habits are driven by our beliefs and assumptions about the world around us. Three months is typically how long it takes for people to unlearn their old beliefs and rewrite new ones – ones that underpin your Customer Strategy. Three months of commitment from the leaders will send a clear message: 'This is here to stay. This is how we do things around here now.'

Measure

The measurement system is one of the most important business systems in your organisation. Note that 'system' here refers not to a piece of technology, but rather to a set of processes and methods that connect together as a system. Measurement gives us feedback on our progress towards our goals and results. Measurement tells us about the efficacy of our Customer Strategy and how well the Architecture for Customer Engagement is working.

Measurement is a key part of the action learning cycle. We need to be able to observe and learn what has worked. Therefore, we need to develop a measurement system that can produce meaningful feedback on how well the different aspects of the Architecture for Customer Engagement are working. As I mentioned earlier, the measurement methodology I use is PuMP®.[67]

Learn

When we receive feedback on the Architecture in the form of measurements and monitoring, we must dedicatedly learn from this. Implementation is iterative. We must mindfully and continually consider how we can finetune the Customer Strategy and Architecture for Customer Engagement to maximise the value of our customer portfolio.

Design

Now, we use what we have learned to finetune the design. We implement these new changes, measure and monitor, learn, and repeat. Then repeat again. In doing so, we continue to make improvements over time. Improving the value of the customer portfolio should become a key part of your day-to-day job. By taking a continuous-improvement approach to incrementally finetuning your tactics, you will build a customer portfolio full of profitable promoters.

Summary

We have used the Architecture for Customer Engagement as our design approach, recognising all the elements that need to be considered and defined beforehand. This design covers who we bring into our customer portfolios and how, as well as how we continue that engagement with our customers. It brings our Customer Strategy to life for the first time.

In this chapter, we looked at the secondary stage of the Architecture for Customer Engagement, considering four stages of customer acquisition: *Attract*, *Get to Know*, *Open Up*, and *Delight*. In particular, we went into more detail on the flow of engagement for B2C and B2B customers. Everything we do in this secondary stage is with the aim of opening a relationship with someone that will become an advocate.

We saw that the implementation of the Architecture is essentially an ongoing process of refinement of the Customer Strategy and Architecture for Customer Engagement, with the long-term goal of improving the value of the customer portfolio from the complementary perspectives of lifetime value and advocacy.

The next chapter will go into more detail on the implementation of strategy. Then, in the appendix, you will find three case studies that will give you more insight into how to develop and apply your Customer Strategy, supported by the Architecture for Customer Engagement, in different contexts.

———

Download these templates to aid you in the development of your Architecture for Customer Engagement.

1. Identifying your Awesome Business Customer Template

2. Values Based Engagement Template

3. Four Stages of B2B Engagement Template

4. The Architecture for Customer Engagement Template.

5. Architecture for Customer Engagement Worksheet

CHAPTER TEN
IMPLEMENT YOUR CUSTOMER STRATEGY WITH PURPOSE

Implementing with purpose

In business and strategy we are told that execution is everything. Quite often we hear that a poor strategy delivered well is far better than a great strategy not implemented at all. When it comes to implementation, I often go back to something I learned during completing my MBA – this quote by Canadian Academic Henry Mintzberg:[68]

> In practice, of course, all strategy making walks on two feet, one deliberate, the other emergent. For just as purely deliberate strategy making precludes learning, so purely emergent strategy making precludes control. Pushed to the limit, neither approach makes much sense.

We start out with a *deliberate and planned strategy*, and over time we end up with a *realised strategy*. This strategy – the one we have implemented – will not perfectly match our original intentions, because through the process of implementation, *emergent strategy* appears. New insights and ideas appear that were not clear before, some of which we choose to integrate into our implementation. Through the sheer limitation of capacity, we drop some portions of strategy to make room for the chosen emergent strategy. Our realised strategy becomes the sum of what we started with and what we elected to add as we implemented, less what we chose to let go. No matter how good our intentions, the strategy we implement or realise will always differ from what we started out with. Sometimes this is for the better, others times not so much.

The development of Customer Strategy is, as I have repeatedly stated, an iterative process. When we first formulate our customer groups and the two-way value exchange, everything will seem quite clear. However, over time our perspective on these groups and their values will sharpen, and the Customer Strategy may need tweaking. This is fine. It fits in with the idea of emergent strategy.

The critical question, then, is *how* you make the decisions about what 'emergent ideas' to allow into your implementation, and what parts of your initial Customer Strategy to drop.

I'd like to suggest two ways to keep implementation on track and realise the best from your Customer Strategy.

1. Use your Customer Strategy and its purpose – to build a more profitable customer portfolio – as a guidebook for your implementation.
2. Develop a measurement system for the outcomes you seek from the implementation.

Let's discuss these in a bit more detail.

Use your Customer Strategy as a guidebook for implementation and change

Your Customer Strategy is not a one-off implementation exercise. It is ongoing, adaptive, and iterative. As you go through the initial roll-out, your Customer Strategy will be finetuned and adapted. However, be sure you stay true to its purpose of building a more valuable customer portfolio. After this first roll-out, follow through is critical, as it will take time for the Customer Strategy – and all the behaviours and decision making that support it – to mature in your business.

If your organisation is coming from a product-centric approach there will be dozens of keystone habits, beliefs, and behaviours that will challenge not only your initial implementation, but also the ongoing maturation of your approach to improving the value of your customer portfolio.

Initially, new projects and products are likely to detract from the Customer Strategy, primarily because the culture of the organisation will still be rooted in those old, product-centric mindsets. It will take time to ensure all efforts are contributing to the goal growing the profitability of the customer portfolio. Dedicated leadership will be needed to steer the Customer Strategy and this new approach towards your 'realised strategy'.

Some organisations decide to use a customer relationship management (CRM) system to help track their engagement with customers. Many organisations initiate a customer experience program. Your Customer Strategy is the guidebook for that program, as it defines the customer groups and what your business has decided to do with each group. Your Customer Strategy should be at the basis of all new systems and changes to operations.

Many organisations appoint a leader to guide the business through the early phases of implementation and keep everything on track. If you have the resources, this is a great approach. Also, businesses often discover that they lack skill in collecting and managing customer data. You may need to invest in building your customer data and analytics capabilities. The 'gold' is often within the insights and hypotheses that come from mining the customer information you have. Skilled data scientists are an asset that will complement the ongoing development of your Customer Strategy and Architecture for Customer Engagement. Over time these capabilities, which are a key part of improving the value of your customer portfolio, will become more deeply integrated into your business and its culture.

Develop a measurement system

Your measurement system is one of the key systems in your business, because the decisions you make will be based on what your measurement system is telling you. When it comes to the implementation stage of a project, we often set ourselves a budget and timeline. This is fine for a project, but not for your Customer Strategy, which will be ongoing. It is better to define the outcomes you seek, then design performance measures that will provide feedback on your progress towards those outcomes.

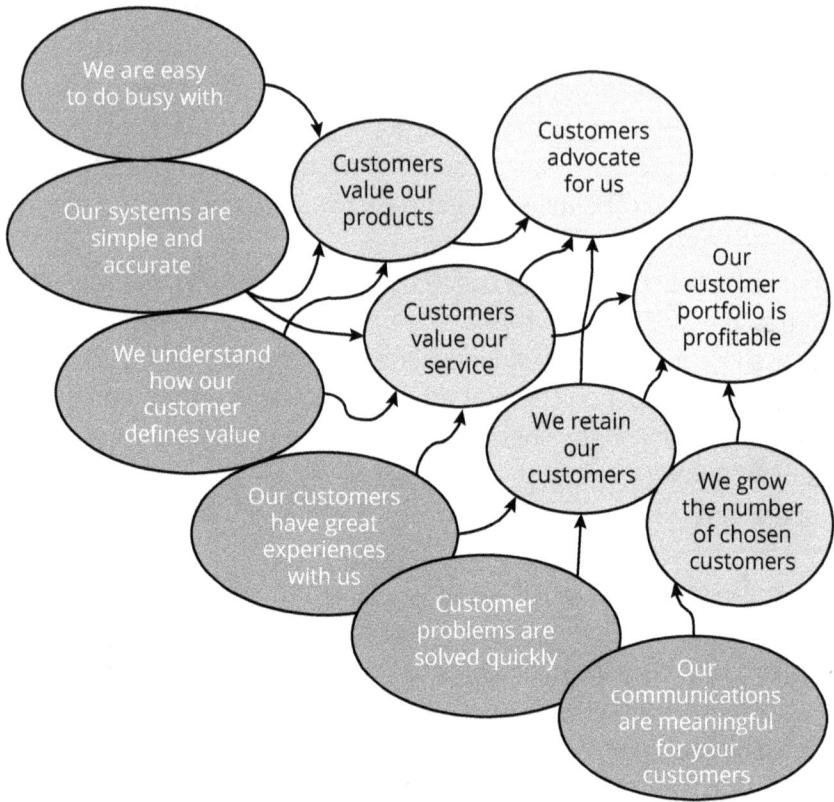

Again, the performance measurement method I use is PuMP®.[69] Within this approach, we first determine what outcomes or results we want to measure. Then we insert these results into the centre of a causal 'results map', and add cause-and-effect relationships that flow in towards the results. This illustration shows a portion of a results map that flows into two results: 'Customers advocate for us', and 'Our customer portfolio is profitable.'

Once we have decided on the results we seek, the PuMP method provides a technique for designing measures for these results. These performance measures will provide feedback on the progress being made, which provides insights into the impact our efforts are having on the specific result. If we wanted, we could add targets to chosen measures, but making progress towards the result is our main goal.

The results map and performance measures provide a framework to assess your progress towards your desired results. This can become your measurement system, the one your turn to when you need to make decisions.

My purpose here is to encourage you to move away from using measures and KPIs in the traditional way. Don't just measure that your actions are complete, or that the project is delivered. Define the outcomes or results you seek, then use performance measures to understand the impact of your actions and projects on those results. Your learnings from using results and measures in this way will help you unlock more and more of the value in your customer portfolio – sooner, and on purpose.

Managing the change

Much has been written on this topic, and there are many approaches out there.[70] But I would just like to share a couple of tips to help you with your change efforts. Firstly, Jeffrey Hiatt's ADKAR model is quite useful in terms of recognising that there is a sequence in change and therefore a sequence in how we communicate, provide training and coaching, and step up to any resistance.[71] Change begins with *Awareness* of the need to change, followed by a *Desire* to change. After the awareness and desire are in place, people must then develop the *Knowledge* and *Ability* to make the change. Once the change is made, they will need to overcome their *Resistance* to this change – their natural tendency to go back to their old ways. We need to recognise that change is individual. One person at a time, and for each person at a different pace. It is only when enough individuals have adopted a change that we can claim to have achieved organisational change.

The second tip I'd like to share is about how to overcome a problem I see regularly with communication. Communication is a key tool in the process of allowing people to buy in to change. But many businesses and organisations seem to form silos. From my observations, in organisational change there are two primary silos: the leadership team or top level of management, who seem to think that change is easy and everyone will get it quickly; and everyone else. When communicating the reason for the change (in order to build awareness and desire), leaders often try to push the messages through the lines of management. Inevitably, somewhere in the mid-levels, the messages get stuck or lost.

I encourage you to adopt what I call the ABCD of communicating change in organisations of any size. In the change effort, the role of a leader or manager is to:

- **A**ctively and visibly support the Customer Strategy and the change
- **B**uild a coalition of support for the change effort through formal and informal networks
- **C**ommunicate directly with frontline employees about the change and the Customer Strategy
- **D**istribute messages, communications, and information about the change to direct reports and team members.

We want to drive messages through the structure to ensure people are hearing it from their direct manager. We also need leaders to communicate directly with frontline people so that we can create a pull effect through the structure as well.

Change takes time. When you think you have implemented and the change is in place, don't stop – keep going for another three months. Leaders always underestimate the time it takes for new organisational habits and beliefs to form.

Building customer engagement capability

Taking an implementation approach like this means accepting that our capability – in engaging with the customer and building our customer portfolio purposefully – will grow over time. We call this *organisational capability* – the ability of the whole organisation in developing a customer portfolio with the purpose of improving business value. All the systems, processes, habits, and skills within the business come together to form this capability.

It's useful to think about this in terms of five levels of organisational maturity in the capability of customer engagement. Let's have a quick look at each level.

Five Levels of Customer Engagement

5	**On purpose**	• Customer acquisition driven by Customer Strategy (Awesome Customer (AC) known) • Revenue / profitability is predictable • Processes / systems enable customer engagement	• Leaders focus on results – purpose is customer focused • Employees engaged • NPS strong for ACs • Increasing AC retention
4	**Almost there**	• Revenue / profitability appears stable • Integrated customer functions and goals • Clear understanding of good leads (MQL/SQL)	• Leaders focus on targets – purpose is company focused • Personas developed • NPS used (overall) • Developing collaboration / skills
3	**Middle of the road**	• Revenue / profitability appears stable but sometimes unexplainable • Separate marketing and sales functions, driven by targets • Processes / systems in development and to be integrated • Leaders focus on targets – purpose is company focused	
2	**Ad Hoc**	• Staff are highly skilled at creating interesting reasons for poor results • Lost sales are about price • Moderate sales team turnover	• "Noisy" customers • Targets are money driven • Blend of Product and Customer focus • Features selling (some advantages)
1	**Exit Strategy**	• Sales results are random • No process or method • Non-productive relationships, • stress and worry	• Targets are money driven • Product is main focus • Leaders are "Gee Men" • Features selling

Level 1: Exit strategy

Imagine yourself walking into a business and asking how things work around here, particularly when it comes to customer engagement. People start telling you that sales are a bit random and unpredictable, mainly because customers can be difficult and they find it hard to differentiate their product in the marketplace. You learn that salespeople are selected based on past experience in the industry and there is no business process about customer engagement. Higher-level staff say things like, 'We rely on people to know what they have to do with the customer' or 'People bring their own skills and they know how to apply them best, we allow them to be themselves...' Targets are financial – revenue targets, or minimal margins, or numbers of units sold. When things are rough and the pressure is on, the leaders start 'geeing' their staff up. This typically starts with 'encouragement – 'You can do this!' – then moves on to 'You better do this – or else.'

I call this level 'exit strategy' because, in my experience, businesses at this level had better either start to work up the maturity scale, or develop an exit strategy for the business.

Level 2: Ad hoc

At the next level up, people are a bit more skilled in describing what's happening, or at least they develop good rhetoric about it. This is a product-centric business that defines the features of the product and expects customers to buy based on how fast they can pitch and close. There is no disciplined approach to engaging customers. The business believes the 'sales gun' myth (see Chapter 3). The sales team has a very high rate of turnover, and the paragon of success is seen as finding a hero to save them.

When sales are lost it is always about price, or some competitor that undercut them. When a sale is won, it is about the relationship. Sorry folks, you can't have it both ways. Losing customers due to price is always an excuse – you just did not explain the value. Customers are often 'noisy' when they did not get the value they thought they were getting.

A business at this level is performing in an ad hoc manner. They need to move up in maturity level or they will continue to feel like victims of the market and their finicky customers.

Level 3: Middle of the road

Middle-of-the-road organisations will survive if they are lucky, but if another business has an eye on the same customers they will eventually be in trouble. They have some systems and processes, but they don't really come together to build a consistent approach to engagement or delivery of value. There might be signs of individuals doing well, but there is no organisational capability. Customers often see the people as the heroes, and will likely follow them onto the next business if they leave. Leaders believe that target setting gets results. The purpose of coming to work is about the business itself – 'We need to make money' or 'We want to be number one in our industry.' No mention of the customer!

At this level the business does not quite realise that an organisation's success lies in how their customers feel about them. When they add the right customers to their customer portfolio, it is by chance. Positive word of mouth seems random, and customer retention is typically a result of the customer not yet having found an alternative. Moving up in maturity level will reap significant benefits for this business.

Level 4: Almost there

Organisations at this level have developed some business-level skills in marketing. They have defined customers as 'personas' but they haven't yet transitioned to understanding true engagement. Marketing and sales are still overwhelmingly seen as something that is 'done to' personas. Marketing and sales might be collaborating to achieve goals, but when the pressure is on this can still break down into internal blame games about the quality of marketing- or sales-qualified leads, which only reduces value. The overall goals are still about the business itself. Success is when the business achieves, not the customer.

For the business at this level, a subtle but important shift will help them move to level 5 and reap the rewards. While the business has capability in marketing and sales, it is not enough to create a customer portfolio full of profitable promoters. Internal success is still about achievement at a silo or divisional level. Developing a Customer Strategy will help unite the teams around a common focus and set of goals.

Level 5: On purpose

When you visit this business and ask them how things work around here, you hear them talk about specific types of customers. They describe the value they need to deliver for these customers so that the customers choose to stay with them and tell their networks about the value they receive. Their purpose in coming to work is to deliver value for *their* awesome customers. All the processes and systems align to deliver that value. People use similar language as they tell stories about awesome customers they have helped and what those customers said.

The leaders are cool and composed, like conductors of an orchestra. They know their role is to support everyone else to do their role the best they can. They know that they are facilitators in bringing all these people and processes together to deliver a harmonic balance for their customers. That is organisational success. The leaders are clear about results they seek and know that they are in a symbiotic relationship with their customers, their audience. They can only succeed when they deliver success for their customers.

––––––

As you develop, implement, and finetune your Customer Strategy over time, look for clues that you are progressing up the maturity scale. All of the indicators within these five levels are observable – you can see and hear them. Take encouragement that progress is being made. Celebrate each small step towards improved levels of organisational customer engagement capability. Doing so will guide you towards on-purpose development of a customer portfolio that is full of profitable promoters.

Summary

In this final chapter, we looked at ways to implement the new Customer Strategy with purpose. Every action should be guided by the Customer Strategy, and supported with a solid system for measuring progress towards the goal of that strategy, that is, creation of a profitable customer portfolio full of promoters.

The process of change must be carefully managed over many months in order to overcome ingrained existing belief structures. During the transition, the ABCD of communicating change can help speed up and improve adoption of the new strategy and process:

- **A**ctively and visibly support the Customer Strategy and the change
- **B**uild a coalition of support for the change
- **C**ommunicate directly with frontline employees
- **D**istribute messages, communications, and information about the change.

Finally, we considered how to assess where your business currently stands in terms of its *organisational capability*, the ability of the whole organisation – its systems, processes, habits, and skills – to come together in developing a customer portfolio with the purpose of improving business value. We looked at five levels of 'maturity' in this regard – *exit strategy, ad hoc, middle of the road, almost there*, and the ultimate aim – *on purpose*.

The final summary

So there you have it.

The secret to designing your business for profit is out. The long-term value is in your customer portfolio. You now have the tools, techniques and templates to unlock that value.

Follow this process to create your Customer Strategy:

1. Identify your various customer groups.
2. Develop an understanding of the two-way value exchange. What do your customers value and need from you, and what value do they reciprocate to you?
3. Select an intent for each customer group. Which represents the best two-way value exchange? This is the group (or groups) to *Grow*. Which groups will you need to *Re-engineer*? Which will you just *Maintain*?

Now develop your level 1 and level 2 value propositions for each of these customer groups. Remember, your communication with your chosen customers has to resonate at a values and an emotional level.

Finally, using your Customer Strategy, start the implementation. Finetune your Architecture for Customer Engagement, and improve your delivery of value.

*   Change your engagement practice to ensure your customer portfolio changes and grows the way you want it to.
*   Finetune service and experience management to support your customer portfolio goals.
*   Ensure all communications (marketing, brand, website – everything) underpins your value propositions and resonates with your chosen customer groups.

- Make sure you have alignment across all your resources and touchpoints to consistently deliver value for your customers. This is the optimal way to achieve a long-term two-way exchange of value with chosen customer groups within your portfolio.

- Measure the impact of your efforts on the results you have chosen, and finetune over time.

Recognise that you will build your business capability in customer engagement deliberately over time. Build the keystone habits of learning, reflecting, and building your customer portfolio purposefully.

It is now over to you. Start now.

APPENDIX

Case study 1: B2B building supplies business

In this case study, we will focus on the building supplies business discussed in the book. This organisation is a wholesale producer of materials used in the domestic and commercial construction industry. Their customers are either merchants who on-sell the products or 're-purposers' who take the products and process them into value-added products for their customers. They have a national sales force supported by distribution centres and small customer service teams. This business is one of three large organisations that dominate the market with about 25–30% market share each (with the remainder picked up by smaller niche producers).

Prior to developing a Customer Strategy, this business used the typical industry approach of hiring people that knew the industry so that they could 'get up to speed' quickly. Salespeople were professional visitors who called on customers regularly and were rewarded based on the number of orders they obtained and the number of new customers they acquired.

The leaders knew they were in a spot of bother when they saw that the number of customers was rising, the number of orders was rising, and everyone was really busy... but revenue was not increasing, and margin even seemed to be dropping. They decided to take a step back and consider the mix of their customer portfolio. They developed a Customer Strategy so that they could increase the profitability of the business by improving the value of the customers they served.

Customer groups

The initial breakdown of customer groups was straightforward, with just two types of customer. Then it became obvious that business size had a significant impact on how the business behaved as a customer. Larger organisations, which often had more disciplined processes and a structure of management, tended to make more formal purchasing decisions, often led by policy rather than personality. In analysing business size as a determinant of customer groups, it became clear fairly quickly that what mattered was the total size of the business, not the size of its transactions. This might seem obvious, but to a building supplies business that was focused on 'orders', the frameshift was significant.

The first challenge for the national sales team was to determine the size of each customer business, and also a 'wallet size'. How much did each business spend per month on products that could be supplied by them? Five customer groups were developed based on business size, from A (largest) through to E (smallest).

Next, we looked into customer behaviours that might produce different decision making and/or demonstrate a different perception of value. We discovered that customers could be divided into three categories:

- Customers with a price bias. These customers were more focused on price than the aspects of service or developing a partnership. These customers wanted a deal each time, either on volume or a lower-quality product, to get the best price they could. They would often play a couple of suppliers off against each other to get the best deal.

- Customers that were more concerned with service than price. Price was important, but getting the right quality and quantity delivered at the right time was far more important than saving a few dollars.

- Customers that were interested in developing a partnership relationship. They valued a relationship that meant their business was being supported by the capability of the supplying business.

Because these descriptors were based on behaviours, it was easy for the national sales team to categorise the customers into each of these groups.

Two-way value exchange

Once we had the customers categorised, we analysed the two-way value exchange as follows.

Customer Group	Value to Customer	Value to Business
Price Bias	• Price • Deals	• Low margin • Higher cost to serve due to protracted negotiations • No positive word of mouth
Service Bias	• Quality products • Reliable supply	• Fair margin • Reasonable cost to serve • Some positive word of mouth
Partnership Bias	• Quality products • Reliable supply • Longer-term commitments for supply • Inventory management at agreed levels	• Good margins • Reasonable cost to serve • Positive word of mouth • Greater confidence in forecast of demand

Value propositions

The level 1 value proposition – about the commitment the business had to the industry, supported by local values, tenure in the industry, and ownership of the business – resonated with customers.

Level 2 value propositions were created for each customer type on the basis of the two-way value exchange above. (The following VPs are paraphrased; product-level VPs were also used as needed.)

- Price Bias: We will quickly provide you with the best available price based on product and volume, so you can make your decision quickly.

- Service Bias: We guarantee the quality of our products and commit to provide you with service you can rely on.

- Partnership Bias: We commit to be your supplier of choice and will support your capability with ours.

Customer intent

After looking at the various customer groups on the basis of type, bias, and business size, the leaders determined the following customer intents for various customer groups (simplified).

- A/B/C size, Partnership Bias – *Grow*.

- A/B/C size, Service Bias – *Grow*.
  (Prioritise a few to *Reengineer* towards Partnership focus)

- Any size, Price Bias – *Maintain*.

- (Prioritise a few of A/B size to *Reengineer* towards Service focus)

Customer Strategy matrix

As the above customer intents were implemented, the national sales team became more of a 'customer account management' team with the larger customers. Systems and processes were developed to support the transition. The *Maintain* intent for the Price Bias customers translated into a transactional approach to service. Quotes were provided quickly with very little negotiations, and offers were sometimes made directly for specific product lines these customers often bought.

The Customer Strategy was translated into a matrix (below), which provided a roadmap with a common language and approach across the whole organisation. This Customer Strategy matrix was used at three levels of customer size – A, B, and C. The idea was to originally to use the matrix for all customers, but we soon realised there was not much long-term value in putting effort into the D and E customers. These customers either shifted to phone-based service, or became a customer of an A or B customer.

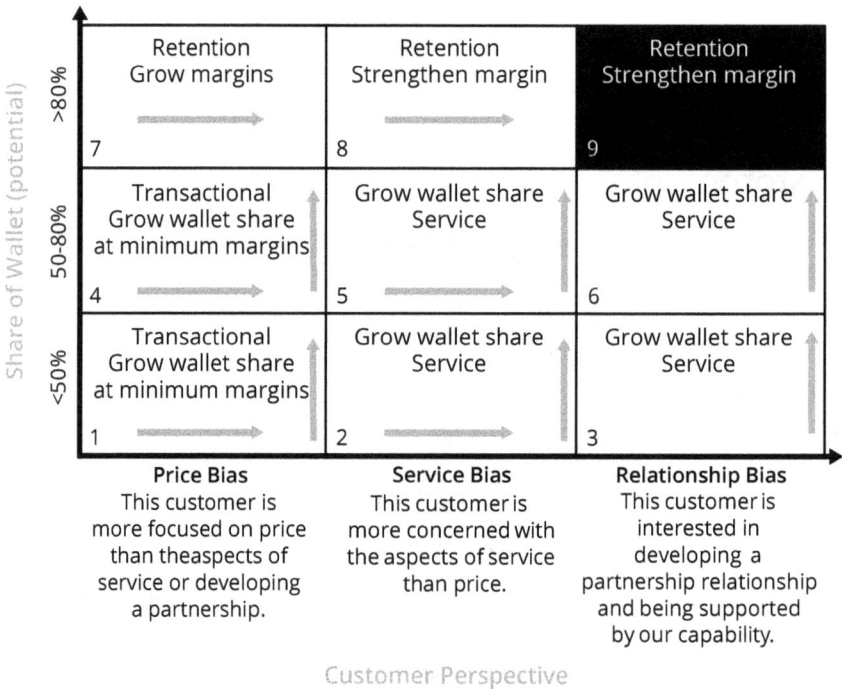

Share of Wallet (potential)	Price Bias	Service Bias	Relationship Bias
>80%	Retention Grow margins 7	Retention Strengthen margin 8	Retention Strengthen margin 9
50-80%	Transactional Grow wallet share at minimum margins 4	Grow wallet share Service 5	Grow wallet share Service 6
<50%	Transactional Grow wallet share at minimum margins 1	Grow wallet share Service 2	Grow wallet share Service 3
	Price Bias This customer is more focused on price than theaspects of service or developing a partnership.	**Service Bias** This customer is more concerned with the aspects of service than price.	**Relationship Bias** This customer is interested in developing a partnership relationship and being supported by our capability.

Customer Perspective

Using the Customer Strategy matrix, customers of each size (A, B, C) were further classified on the basis of their bias and share of wallet. A customers became A1 (bottom left corner) to A9 (top right corner) customers, B became B1 to B9, and so on. This became the new language within the business. Discussions became about how to *Grow* an A2 into an A5 or an A3. The customer pathway towards A9 was mapped out, and so were the tactical approaches for account managers.

Results

Almost immediately the business became more profitable.

- The cost of service (time and effort) to Price Bias customers decreased, as did the number of orders at low margins.
- Within a relatively short period of time, share of wallet of the larger Partnership and Service Bias customers increased.
  - Delivery of value to these customers increased.
  - Service cost per customer decreased, as a smaller portion of customers were receiving deliveries.
  - Margins improved.
- Over a longer period of time, another benefit emerged. The other two market-dominating organisations maintained their approach and lost value from the industry. The business that adopted the Customer Strategy was able to extract more value from the market. More and more, the Price Bias customers harassed the other two players to get the deals they wanted.

Comments from sales team members and customer account managers

- 'Working together as a team [salespeople and manager] has produced communication and problem solving so that we are coming up with better approaches to the customer account. Working as a team I come up with better ideas than I could on my own.'
- 'The process is difficult to get your head around initially, but once you do, it really changes your perception on what you do. It is not about getting to see as many people as you can, but about thinking about who to see and what to say when you get there.'
- 'Using the planning techniques allowed me to realise who my customers were, who had the most potential – and also how little I actually knew about them...'

Comments from leaders and managers

- 'It was difficult to get the process going at first, but eventually it took hold. The reps now have a purpose with their call on the customer. Before this they may have called on the customer and chatted about various topical things, but now they are focused on understanding their customers' business. As a result of this approach one of our reps was told by the customer that we were difficult to do business with – we responded to the issues and the customer's sales have gone through the roof! This has happened with three other customers as well.'

- 'Our reps used to service up to 70 customers. So, what they would do is try to get around to as many as possible – but now they focus on planning and growing share of wallet with their higher-value and higher-potential customers. They now feel that this is manageable. They are also having more success in developing 'partner' style relationships. With these things combined together, an improvement in their confidence and motivation is really noticeable.'

- 'We got some resistance from the reps but persevered with the principles behind the Customer Strategy, share of wallet, grading by potential, and customer account planning mainly. Over the last eight months we have been able to grow our market share by 14%. For years we had been unable to shift it (market share), but by using a disciplined, planned approach we have achieved what I did not think we could.'

- 'The benefits of using the process have been phenomenal. Our net profit for the branch is up 30%. One of the benefits we didn't expect is that you can reduce costs by focusing the reps' activity on the higher-potential customers.'

Case Study 2: Amazon

In this case study, we will take Amazon as an example of how building and implementing a Customer Strategy can deliver long-term profitability and advocacy.

As you may know, Amazon's vision has always been to be 'Earth's most customer-centric company' for four primary customer sets: consumers, sellers, enterprises, and content creators.[72] It's a very clear vision that everyone in the business can understand. Additionally, they have recognised that customers are not one big amorphous group, but specific customer groups (and undoubtedly subgroups) with specific needs.

Since its inception in 1997, Amazon has always said, 'We will continue to focus relentlessly on our customers', believing that this focus would produce the desired long-term results... and it has.[73] This relentless focus continues today and is now described as 'true customer obsession'.[74] The following is from Jeff Bezos, in his introduction to the 2016 Amazon Annual Report.[75]

> There are many ways to center a business. You can be competitor focused, you can be product focused, you can be technology focused, you can be business model focused, and there are more. But in my view, obsessive customer focus is by far the most protective of Day 1 vitality.
>
> Why? There are many advantages to a customer-centric approach, but here's the big one: customers are always beautifully, wonderfully dissatisfied, even when they report being happy and business is great. Even when they don't yet know it, customers want something better, and your desire to delight customers will drive you to invent on their behalf. No customer ever asked Amazon to create the Prime membership program, but it sure turns out they wanted it, and I could give you many such examples.
>
> Staying in Day 1 requires you to experiment patiently, accept failures, plant seeds, protect saplings, and double down when you see customer delight. A customer-obsessed culture best creates the conditions where all of that can happen.

To me there are (at least) three powerful points that come from this statement:

1. Being focused on the customer will always allow you to remain relevant for your customers. This in turn can lead to a more profitable customer portfolio and greater levels of advocacy.

2. Being centred on customers allows people within the business to connect more with the vision and collectively work towards it.

3. The last two sentences are really about an organisational culture focused on improving customer value and business performance. People within the business can only feel that it is okay to experiment, fail, learn, and test against 'customer delight', when they know their leaders are similarly committed.

In 2018, Amazon became one of the world's largest businesses and the USA's second (behind Apple) trillion-dollar company.[76] This is all thanks to their long-term approach and strategy. Value for customers delivers value for the organisation in the long run.

Surprisingly, in a recent interview, Jeff Bezos said that he believes that one day Amazon will fail, just like all large organisations. Amazon's job, he said, is 'to delay failure for as long as possible by focusing on its customers. If we start to focus on ourselves, instead of focusing on our customers, that will be the beginning of the end. We have to try and delay that day for as long as possible.'[77]

Customer groups and the two-way value exchange

Amazon serves four main customer groups: Consumers, Sellers, Content Creators, and Enterprises. (An 'Enterprise' customer is a B2B organisation that Amazon provides technology solutions for.) Here we will focus on the first three groups.

Customer Group	Value to Customer	Value to Amazon
Consumers	• Lower prices every day • Large selection • Customer reviews • Convenience • Positive experience • Fast, reliable fulfilment	• Working capital • Revenue from the margin on sales • Positive word of mouth • Consumer traffic for Sellers and Content Creators • Customer data
Subgroup: Prime Subscribers	• Prime membership program • Exclusive access to content	• Subscriptions • More customer data
Sellers and Content Creators	• Access to consumers • Product sales • Product pages • Creator profiles, videos, and social media	• Inventory to offer Consumers • Revenue from the margin on sales

The two-way value exchange here has a beautiful quality to it. All three key entities – Consumers, Sellers, and Amazon – enjoy wonderful benefits and value from the ongoing relationship. From Amazon's perspective, they need to deliver value for Sellers so that they can attract Consumers, and also attract Consumers so that Sellers will list their products. By creating this value exchange between these two customer groups, Amazon is able to generate long-term value from its customer portfolio.

Value propositions

The overarching value propositions could be described as follows.

Consumers	• Everything you want from A to Z • Trusted payments • Guaranteed delivery, and we'll fix it if something goes wrong
Sellers and Content Creators	• Reach hundreds of millions of customers • Let us do the heavy lifting for you (fulfilment services) • Get your products seen by more shoppers (advertising services)

Customer intent

From these customer groups and the value exchange, we can see the core intent is to *Grow* the number of both Consumers and Sellers. This was Amazon's intent from the beginning, but a Customer Strategy is iterative. As the volume of Consumers has grown, new products and services have been added, which has created additional sub-groups, such as Amazon Prime Subscribers. The same principle would apply to the Sellers and Content Creators.

Results

The result of implementing, redefining, and reinventing the Customer Strategy is a customer portfolio that provides significant value – to the point where, in the long run, Amazon has become one of the largest businesses in the world.

Case Study 3: Government-owned, non-profit electricity company

Just like other organisations, most government agencies or non-profits exist to serve customers. An organisation can still benefit from applying the principles of *Profit by Design* even it is not for profit. Defining your customer groups and understanding the value exchange between you and each customer group, and even between customer groups, can add enormous insight into how you deliver value. Making deliberate decisions on how to create value can provide much needed clarity and perspective.

In this case study, we will follow a government-owned agency responsible for distribution of electricity to the community. This power network oversees energy flow from generators, through high-voltage transmission lines, into the distribution network, and on to the consumer. The agency had resolved to be 'customer driven' in all it did, but it was still seeing 'the customer' as anyone and everyone. They sought to develop a Customer Strategy to unlock insights into how to be more customer driven.

Customer groups

Two broad customer groups immediately emerged: customers the agency deliver value *to*, and customers they deliver value *through*. Within these groups, four core customer groups were defined:

1. End Consumers (deliver value to)

2. Government (deliver value to)

3. Electricity Retailers (deliver value through)

4. Partners (deliver value through).

Subgroups were then developed and further defined for each core customer group.

1. End Consumers
   a. Residential
   b. Small Business
   c. Medium Business
   d. Large Business
2. Government (shareholder)
3. Electricity Retailers (sellers of electricity and energy solutions)
4. Partners (in the delivery of value to customers)
   a. Electrical Contractors
   b. Inverter Energy System Providers
   c. Developers (housing, commercial, and industrial estates)
   d. Aggregators (who manage and/or demand on behalf of a group of customers)
   e. Community and Industry Groups (lobbyists)
   f. Our People (employees of the distributor)

Two-way value exchange and customer intent

Initially, the two-way value exchange seemed pretty straightforward: the distributor provided access to electricity. But in reality the value exchange was more complex. It seems to me that in organisations we often tend to oversimplify the complex to make it easier to deal with. However, the solution is always in unpacking the complexity and understanding the relationships that come together to make this ecosystem of value exchange thrive.

The following table shows how the value exchange was unpacked for the group End Consumers – Residential. (Each customer group/subgroup was unpacked in the same way.)

End Consumers – Residential	
Role	Users and producers of energy
	Adopters of competing technologies and products
Core needs	Affordability – leaving money for other things/ability to pay bills
	Choice and control – of tariffs and technology
	Peace of mind – reliability of supply to maintain lifestyle
What they value	A proactive, friendly electricity partner who provides:
	• a reliable, affordable and safe electricity supply
	• timely connection and restoration services
	• communication on outages, restoration times and works progress
	• installation of inverter energy systems and other technologies.
Customer Strategy (customer intent)	*Re-engineer* the relationship.
	Transform the way the customer interacts with us so that ultimately (over 2–3 years) we become an essential enabler for customers' energy needs and are able to effectively manage network demand.
	This strategy effectively develops a collaborative relationship with customers to enable relevant solutions both on-grid and beyond the meter.

Results

A detailed model was formed that mapped the value exchange between the distributor and the various customer groups. With a clear understanding of these relationships and of the value exchange, intentional strategies were deployed to enhance the exchange of value and improve the value of the whole ecosystem for all parties.

For example, the distributor ran a Voice-of-the-Customer survey program, which really focused on the End Consumers group (predominantly Residential). Overall, measures indicated that the sentiment towards the distributor in this large customer group was not particularly favourable. The organisation's initial reaction was to launch a communication initiative to inform these customers of what a great job they were really doing for them. But when it came to developing a budget for the communication plan the numbers were a bit frightening, and a return on investment was not guaranteed.

A fresh look at the value exchange between the customer groups highlighted that that main influencer for Residential customers (in forming their opinions of the distributor) were Electrical Contractors (ECs), who were giving negative word of mouth. An examination of why ECs felt as they did highlighted poor communication with and support for ECs. Effort was put into improving performance in these areas, and the flow-on effect was that ECs began to change the language they used with their Residential customers. In the main, they spoke more favourably of the distributor, which in turn changed the sentiments of the Residential customer group.

The cost of improving delivery of value to ECs was a fraction of the cost of the planned communication program for the Residential customers. The implemented changes delivered multiple operational benefits, including lower costs to serve ECs, quick turnaround time on jobs, and faster problem resolution. And those improvements in turn delivered benefits to the Residential customer group as well.

By focusing on their customer portfolio, this government agency improved value delivery to their customer groups. In other words, they achieved profit by design in a non-profit environment.

TEMPLATES

Here is a set of Templates to assist you with creating your customer portfolio full of profitable promoters.

Templates for Chapter 5
Identifying Customer Groups Template
Customer Value Map Template
How your Customer Defines Value Template

Templates for Chapter 6
The NPS Calculation Template
eCLV Calculation Template
Intent with a Customer Group Template

Templates for Chapter 7
Level One Value Proposition Template
Level Two Value Proposition Template

Templates for Chapter 8
Adoption (1) Innovation Template
Customer Adoption (2) Template
Values and Behaviours Template
Ethics and Behaviours Template

Templates for Chapter 9

Identifying your Awesome Business Customer Template

Values Based Engagement Template

Four Stages of B2B Engagement Template

The Architecture for Customer Engagement Template

Architecture for Customer Engagement Worksheet

The templates are available to download free at:

www.markhocknell.com/book

NOTES AND REFERENCES

1   McKendrick, N. 1960. "Josiah Wedgwood: An Eighteenth-Century Entrepreneur in Salesmanship and Marketing Techniques." *The Economic History Review* 12, no. 3: 408–433.
2   Ibid.
3   Pink, Daniel H. 2012. *To Sell is Human.* Riverhead Books, USA.
4   For more about the experience economy, I encourage you to look into the work of Joe Pine, in particular: Pine, B. Joseph II and James Gilmore. 2011. *The Experience Economy.* Updated edition. Harvard Business Review Press. See also: Strategic Horizons LLP. 2016. "Joe Pine Overviews the Experience Economy." Uploaded on August 26, 2016. YouTube video, 13:24 min. https://www.youtube.com/watch?v=M7rGBgn9jAl.
5   For a more detailed discussion on the perils of the product-centric approach, see the work of Peter Fader, Professor of Marketing at the Wharton School of the University of Pennsylvania, in particular: Fader, Peter. 2010. *Customer Centricity.* Wharton Digital Press.
6   You can learn more about the CRM project through these articles: Gallagher, Julie. 2002. "Suncorp Obtains Single Customer View." *Insurance and Technology*, 28(1): 20; Lawson, Mark. 2002. "Suncorp Sees System as Key to Allfinanz Strategy." *Australian Financial Review*, July 18, 2002: 20.
7   Moullakis, Joyce. 2003. "Ranks to Cross-Sell for Growth." *Australian Financial Review*, July 4, 2003: 72; Riley, James. 2003. "Suncorp Boosts CRM Cross-Sell." *The Australian*, July 22, 2003: 7; Collins, Kimberly. 2003. "Suncorp Delivers on Allfinanz Strategy Through CRM." GartnerG2 Case Study, June 2003.
8   See Koch, Richard. 1999. *The 80/20 Principle: The Secret to Achieving More with Less.* Doubleday, New York.
9   Bliss, Jeanne. 2006. *Chief Customer Officer.* Jossey-Bass, San Francisco.
10   Ibid.
11   Cave, Andrew. 2017. "Culture Eats Strategy for Breakfast. So What's for Lunch?" Forbes, November 9. https://www.forbes.com/sites/andrewcave/2017/11/09/culture-eats-strategy-for-breakfast-so-whats-for-lunch/#16f1e8437e0f
12   Sharot, Tali. 2017. *The Influential Mind.* Henry Holt and Co.
13   Kohn, Alfie. 1987. "The Case Against Competition." Alfie Kohn, September 1987. https://www.alfiekohn.org/article/case-competition/
14   Sheldon, Arthur Fredrick. 1911. *The Art of Selling.* Kessinger Publishing, Whitefish MT, United States.
15   Wizdo, Lori. 2013. "The New Physics of Lead-Revenue Management." *Forrester*, March 28, 2013. http://docplayer.net/7924503-The-new-physics-of-lead-to-revenue-management.html
16   Smith, Adam. 1776. *Wealth of Nations.* W. Strahan and T. Cadell, London
17   Dixon, Matthew, and Brent Adamson. 2011. *The Challenger Sale.* Portfolio Penguin, London.
18   ISO DESIGN. 2016. "Roman Army Structure | Vindolanda Museum." Uploaded on October 26, 2016. YouTube video, 3:07 min. https://www.youtube.com/watch?v=Rcbedan5R1s
19   Systems thinking was brought into focus for business by Peter Senge. The principles have since been used and applied extensively (e.g., with Six Sigma and lean methods). For more information, see: Senge, Peter. 1990. *The Fifth Discipline.* Random House Australia; Senge, Peter, Art Kleiner, Charlotte Roberts, Richard B. Ross, and Bryan J. Smith. 1994. *The Fifth Discipline Field Book.* Nicholas Brealey Publishing.

20   Lindstrom, Michael. 2009. *Buyology*. This was one of the first published research projects to demonstrate the significant connection between emotions and decision making. Leaders in the field of Behavioural Economics, including Daniel Kahneman, Richard Thaler, Cass Sunstein, and others, have researched and written extensively on emotional and bias-driven decision making. The connection has also been reaffirmed in many books, for example: Levitin, Daniel. 2014. *The Organized Mind*. Random House. Levitin states that "Economic decisions produce activity in the emotional regions of the brain" (p. 276). See also Sharot, Tali. 2017. *The Influential Mind*. Henry Holt and Co.; Pohlmann, Andrew P., Peter E. Steidl, and Stephen J. Genco. 2013. *Neuromarketing For Dummies*. Wiley.

21   Sinek, Simon. 2009. *Start with Why*. Portfolio Penguin, London.

22   For more on organisational habits, see Duhigg, Charles. 2014. *The Power of Habit: Why We Do What We Do in Life and Business*. Random House, USA.

23   Gulati, Ranjay. 2009. *Reorganise for Resilience*. Harvard Business School Press. The Forrester research is summarised in: Manning, Harley, and Kerry Bodine. 2012. *Outside In: The Power of Putting Customers at the Center of Your Business*. 1st edition. Amazon Publishing. Research from the London School of Economics (http://www.lse.ac.uk/) has been valuable in connecting the value of CLV and NPS, for example: Kirby, Justin and Samson, Alain (2008) *Customer advocacy metrics: the NPS theory in practice*. Admap, Feb. pp. 17-19. ISSN 0001-8295; and: Fader, P S and Hardie, B G S (2015) *Simple probability models for computing CLV and CE*. In: Handbook of research on customer equity in marketing.

24   Gulati, *Reorganise for Resilience*. This research assessed businesses both before and after the Global Financial Crisis of 2008.

25   Lindstrom, *Buyology*.

26   Jurevicius, Ovidijus. 2019 "SWOT analysis of Amazon (5 Key Strengths in 2019)." Strategic Management Insight, January 10, 2019. https://www.strategicmanagementinsight.com/swot-analyses/amazon-swot-analysis.html

27   Spaceship. "About Us." Accessed August 1, 2019. https://www.spaceship.com.au/about-us

28   For more on Starbucks' segmentation, targeting, and positioning, see: Dudovskiy, John. 2017. "Starbucks Segmentation, Targeting and Positioning – Targeting Premium Customers with Quality Products and Service." *Research Methodology*, April 17, 2017. https://research-methodology.net/starbucks-segmentation-targeting-and-positioning-targeting-premium-customers-with-quality-products-and-service/

29   The idea of articulating how customers define was first inspired by McKenzie, Ray. 2001. *The Relationship-Based Enterprise*. McGraw-Hill.

30   The value of community is demonstrated on Hubspot Academy's User Groups page: Hubspot. "Hubspot User Groups." Accessed August 1, 2019. https://academy.hubspot.com/hubspot-user-groups - the testimonials provided demonstrate the value of community.

31   News Corp Australia. "Quest Community News." Accessed August 1, 2019. http://www.newscorpaustralia.com/brand/quest-community-news

32   Reichheld, Fred. 1996. *The Loyalty Effect*. Harvard Business School Press.

33   Reichheld, Fred. 2006. *The Ultimate Question: Driving Good Profits and True Growth*. Harvard Business School Press.

34   To see how Telstra improved their NPS, see: Cameron, Nadia. 2017. "Telstra Sees Dip in NPS, Financial Results." CMO, February 16, 2017. https://www.cmo.com.au/article/614369/telstra-sees-dip-nps-financials-increases-customer-base/ ; Cameron, Nadia. 2017. Telstra Reports Strong Financials, NPS Lift." CMO, August 17, 2017. https://www.cmo.com.au/article/626133/telstra-reports-strong-financials-nps-lift/

35   Gupta, Sunil, and Donald R. Lehman. 2005. *Managing Customers as Investments*. Wharton School Publishing.

36   Savage, Sam L. 2012. *The Flaw of Averages*. Wiley.

37   Inspired by: Buttle, Francis, (2009), *Customer Relationship Management: Concepts and Technologies*, Elsevier Butterworth-Heinemann, Oxford

38   Abductive logic is well described by: Martin, Roger. 2009. *The Design of Business*. Harvard Business Press, Boston, pp. 62–68.

39   Maurya, Ash. 2012. *Running Lean: Iterate from Plan A to a Plan That Works*. 2nd edition. O'Reilly Media, p. 29.

40   Anderson, James C., James A. Narus, and Wouter van Rossum. 2006. "Customer Value Propositions in Business Markets." *Harvard Business Review*, 84: 91–99.

41   Dixon, M. and Adamson, B. (2011), *The Challenger Sale*. Penguin Books, London.

42   TechnologyOne website: https://www.technologyonecorp.com/local-government accessed June 19 2019

43   Christensen, Clayton M., Taddy Hall, Karen Dillon, and David S. Duncan. 2016. "Know Your Customers' 'Jobs to Be Done'." *Harvard Business Review*, September 2016. https://hbr.org/2016/09/know-your-customers-jobs-to-be-done ; Strategsys. 2017. "Jobs-to-Be-Done – Prof. Clayton Christensen." Uploaded March 13, 2017. YouTube video, 7:56 min. https://www.youtube.com/watch?v=Q63PZR7mG70

44   Strategyzer. 2019. "Why Use the Value Proposition Canvas?" Strategyzer. Accessed August 1, 2019. https://strategyzer.com/canvas/value-proposition-canvas

45   Sinek, Simon. 2009. "How Great Leaders Inspire Action." TED talk, 17:58 min. https://www.ted.com/talks/simon_sinek_how_great_leaders_inspire_action (the quote occurs between 3 and 5 minutes in)

46   This information was obtained through discussions with Gavin Merriman, then Marketing Manager of Nude by Nature. Further information about their initiative can be found here: Cameron, Nadia. 2016. "An In-Depth Look at Nude by Nature's Data and Personalisation Journey." CMO, July 25, 2016. https://www.cmo.com.au/article/603959/an-in-depth-look-nude-by-nature-data-personalisation-journey/

47   Endeavour Foundation https://www.endeavour.com.au/; and from information presented at the Brand Launch 7th June 2018, Brisbane

48   The features/advantages/benefits scheme is drawn from: Rackham, Neil. 1988. *SPIN Selling*. McGraw-Hill Education, New York.

49   Dixon and Adamson, *The Challenger Sale*.

50   Fender. 2016. "Kenny Wayne Shepherd Introduces the Fender American Professional Stratocaster." Uploaded December 7, 2016. YouTube video, 8:20 min. https://www.youtube.com/watch?v=adqDosE3wCk&t=198s

51   Drucker, Peter. 1973. Management. New York: Harper and Row.

52   Matthews, Byron, and Schenk, Tamara. 2018. *Sales Enablement: A Master Framework to Engage, Equip, and Empower A World-Class Sales Force*. Wiley, p. 131.

53   Spitzer, Dean R. 2007. *Transforming Performance Measurement: Rethinking the Way We Measure and Drive Organizational Success*. Amacom.

54   Learn more about PuMP here: Stacey Barr. "Stacey Barr." Accessed August 1, 2019. www.staceybarr.com. See also: Barr, Stacey. 2014. *Practical Performance Measurement*. Wiley Australia; Barr, Stacey. 2017. *Prove It!* Wiley Australia.

55   Rogers, Everett M. 1983. *Diffusion of Innovation*. 3rd edition. Free Press, New York.

56   Moore, Geoff A. 1991. *Crossing the Chasm: Marketing and Selling Technology Products to Mainstream Customers*. New York: Harper Business.

57   'Nudge' is an allusion to a book from the field of Behavioural Economics: Thayler, Richard, and Cass Sustein. 2008. *Nudge.* Yale University Press. See also: Cialdini, Robert B. 1984. *Influence: How and Why People Agree to Things.* Harper Collins

58   For further consideration of values and ethics, see: Nasirabadi, E.Z., and R. Golestani. 2013. "The Impact of Salesperson and Dealer on Brand Loyalty." *Research Journal of Applied Sciences, Engineering and Technology*, 5 (12): 3306–3311; Lin, S. H., and H. Wu. 2012. "Effects of Ethical Sales Behaviour Considered through Transaction Cost Theory: To Whom Is the Customer Loyal?" *Journal of International Management Studies*, 7 (1): 31–41; Wentzel, D. and S. Henkel. 2009. "The Impact of Employee Behaviour on Brand Personality Impressions: The Moderating Effect of Pseudorelevant Information." *Advances in Consumer Research*, 36.

59   See the following articles for more on the Wells Fargo scandal: Cox, Jeff. 2016. "Wells Fargo Getting Smacked by Wall Street Analysts." *CNBC*, October 5, 2016. https://www.cnbc.com/2016/10/05/wells-fargo-getting-smacked-by-wall-street-analysts-fitch-raymond-james-and-goldman-sachs.html; McGrath, Maggie. 2016. "Warren Buffett On Wells Fargo Fiasco: 'It's A Great Bank That Made A Terrible Mistake'" *Forbes*, November 11, 2016. https://www.forbes.com/sites/maggiemcgrath/2016/11/11/warren-buffett-on-wells-fargo-fiasco-its-a-great-bank-that-made-a-terrible-mistake/#670e145e3304; Blake, Paul. 2016. "Timeline of the Wells Fargo Accounts Scandal." *ABC News*, November 3, 2016. https://abcnews.go.com/Business/timeline-wells-fargo-accounts-scandal/story?id=42231128 ; Shen, Lucinda. 2016. "Wells Fargo's Scandal Could End Up Costing Bank $8 Billion." *Fortune*, October 24, 2016; http://fortune.com/2016/10/24/wells-fargos-scandal-could-end-up-costing-bank-8-billion/ ; Egan, Matt. 2016. "Wells Fargo's Reputation is Tanking, Survey Finds." *CNN Business*, October 24, 2016. https://money.cnn.com/2016/10/24/investing/wells-fargo-fake-accounts-angry-customers/index.html. Egan, Matt. 2016, "5,300 Wells Fargo employees fired over 2 million phony accounts." *CNN Business*, September 6 2016, https://money.cnn.com/2016/09/08/investing/wells-fargo-created-phony-accounts-bank-fees/index.html

60   The full report of the 2018 Financial Services Royal Commission is available at: Australian Government. Royal Commission into Misconduct in the Banking, Superannuation and Financial

Services Industry." Accessed August 1, 2019. https://financialservices.royalcommission.gov.au/
Pages/default.aspx. See also the following articles: Chau, David 2019 "Pitiful payouts' from 'junk'
credit insurance sold by major banks with loans and credit cards" ABC News https://www.abc.net.
au/news/2019-07-11/asic-report-slams-consumer-credit-insurance/11298732; Complispace Report,
2018 "Royal Commission (Part Two): Conflicts of Interest, Remuneration and Intermediaries" https://
www.complispace.com.au/blog/risk-compliance/royal-commission-conflicts-interest-remuneration-
intermediaries/; Australian Government – Treasury 2018, FINANCIAL SERVICES ROYAL COMMISSION,
SUBMISSION HEARINGS ON FINANCIAL ADVICE, accessed https://financialservices.royalcommission.
gov.au/public-hearings/Documents/Round-2-written-submissions/treasury.pdf

61   ABC News. 2018. "Banking Royal Commission: ANZ Chief Says Many Employees 'Dehumanise' Work as
'They Don't See a Customer'." Updated June 30, 2018. http://www.abc.net.au/news/2018-06-30/anz-
chief-says-bank-employees-dehumanise-work-dont-see-customer/9927340

62   Rudin, Andrew. 2018. "Announcing 16 New Inductees to the Sales Ethics Hall of Shame."
CustomerThink, May 8, 2018. http://customerthink.com/announcing-16-new-inductees-to-the-sales-
ethics-hall-of-shame/

63   Bradt, George 2016 "Wanamaker Was Wrong -- The Vast Majority Of Advertising Is Wasted" Forbes,
https://www.forbes.com/sites/georgebradt/2016/09/14/wanamaker-was-wrong-the-vast-majority-of-
advertising-is-wasted/#68b4cecc483b

64   Five by Five. "Get a Plan for a Great Looking, High Performing Website." Accessed August 1, 2019.
https://www.fivebyfive.com.au/website-designer-landing/; and: Hollenberg, Jon (2014) Love at First Site:
how to build the website of your dreams, Five by Five Marketing Pty Ltd

65   Miller, Robert, Stephen Heiman, and Tad Tuleja. 2005. The New Strategic Selling: The Unique Sales
System Proven Successful by the World's Best Companies. Revised edition. Grand Central Publishing.;
Dixon and Adamson, The Challenger Sale.

66   Rackham, SPIN Selling.

67   Stacey Barr, "Stacey Barr."

68   Mintzberg, Henry. 1987. "Crafting Strategy." Harvard Business Review, July 1987. https://hbr.
org/1987/07/crafting-strategy

69   Stacey Barr, "Stacey Barr." For more on performance measurement, visit my website https://www.
markhocknell.com/what-i-do/pump-and-kpis/ and download a copy of the whitepaper The Eight Steps
to a High Performance Organisation.

70   For more on managing change, see: Hiatt, Jeffrey M. and Timothy J. Creasey. 2012. Change
Management: The People Side of Change. Prosci Learning Centre Publications, Colorado.

71   Hiatt, Jeffrey M. 2006. ADKAR: A Model for Change in Business, Government and Our Community. Prosci
Learning Centre Publications, Colorado.

72   Amazon. 2016. 2016 Annual Report. https://ir.aboutamazon.com/static-files/380785a4-779c-4252-
897b-539d3ef70680

73   Hewett, Jennifer. 2017. "Amazon CEO Jeff Bezos' Relentless Customer Focus is the Same 20 Years
On." Financial Review, April 23, 2017. https://www.afr.com/news/economy/amazon-ceo-jeff-bezos-
relentless-customer-focus-is-the-same-20-years-on-20170420-gvp2u6

74   Amazon, 2016 Annual Report.

75   Ibid.

76   DePillis, Lydia. 2018. "Amazon is Now Worth $1,000,000,000,000." CNN Business, September 4, 2018.
https://money.cnn.com/2018/09/04/technology/amazon-1-trillion/index.html

77   Asher Hamilton, Isobel. 2018. "'I predict one day Amazon will fail. Amazon will go bankrupt': Jeff Bezos
makes surprise admission about Amazon's life span." Business Insider Australia, November 16, 2018.
https://www.businessinsider.com.au/jeff-bezos-says-amazon-will-fail-one-day-2018-11?r=US&IR=T

ABOUT THE AUTHOR

Mark Hocknell's experience covers three decades and ranges from corporate line management roles to consulting and academia. Today he specialises in applying a customer centric approach to business and gaining performance improvement through measurement.

Mark led one of the first large-scale CRM deployments for one of Australia's leading financial institutions. He was then asked by the Graduate School of Business (QUT) to develop and teach two courses on the MBA program: Sales Management and Customer Relationship Management. He taught these courses for almost ten years whilst concurrently consulting to organisations of all shapes and sizes. He has an MBA and several certifications including, Net Promoter Score, Prosci (Change Management) and PuMP (Performance Measurement method).

He is based in south-east Queensland with his family and enjoys getting outdoors, especially to the beaches. He has a keen interest in music, travel, history, the environment, and animal welfare.

www.ingramcontent.com/pod-product-compliance
Lightning Source LLC
Chambersburg PA
CBHW071414210326
41597CB00020B/3499